Withdrawn From Stock
Dublin Public Libraries
D1348609

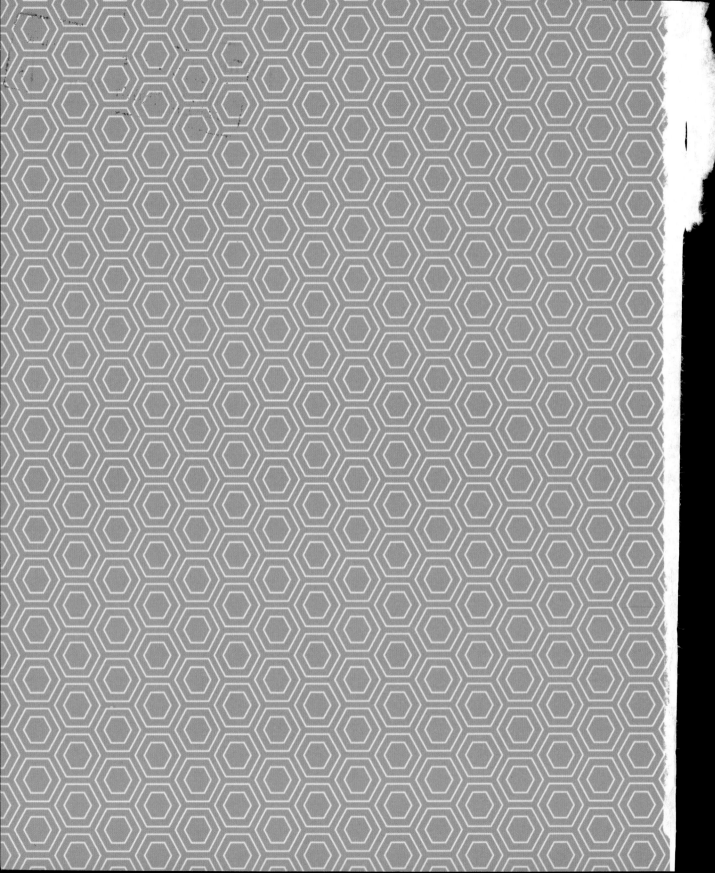

Withdrawn From Stock
Dublin Public Libraries

FESTA

FESTA

A Year of

ITALIAN CELEBRATIONS

– RECIPES AND RECOLLECTIONS –

Eileen Dunne Crescenzi

Brainse Ráth Maonais
Rathmines Branch
Fón / Tel: 4973539

GILL & MACMILLAN

Gill & Macmillan
Hume Avenue
Park West
Dublin 12
www.gillmacmillanbooks.ie

© Eileen Dunne Crescenzi 2015

978 07171 6444 8

Edited by Kristin Jensen
Designed by Fidelma Slattery
Photography © Joanne Murphy
Photos on pp 32, 113, 144, 220 courtesy of
Eileen Dunne Crescenzi; photos on pp 40, 148, 171
© Canstock
Styling by Orla Neligan
Assistants to photographer and stylist:
Liosa MacNamara and Aga Wypych
Indexed by Adam Pozner
Printed by Printer Trento Srl, Italy

PROPS
Avoca: HQ Kilmacanogue, Bray, Co. Wicklow.
T: (01) 2746939; E: info@avoca.ie;
www.avoca.ie

Meadows & Byrne: Dublin, Cork, Galway,
Clare, Tipperary. T: (01) 2804554/(021) 4344100;
E: info@meadowsandbyrne.ie;
www.meadowsandbyrne.com

Eden Home & Garden: 1–4 Temple Grove,
Temple Road, Blackrock, Co. Dublin.
T: (01) 7642004;
E: edenhomeandgarden@hotmail.com;
www.edenhomeandgarden.ie

Dunnes Stores, Cornelscourt: Bray Road,
Foxrock, Dublin 18. T: (01) 2892677;
www.dunnesstores.com

TK Maxx: The Park, Carrickmines, Dublin 18.
T: (01) 2074798; www.tkmaxx.ie

House of Fraser: Dundrum Town Centre,
Dublin 16. T: (01) 2991400;
E: dundrum@hof.co.uk; houseoffraser.co.uk

Harold's Bazaar: 208 Harold's Cross Road,
Dublin 6W. T: (087) 7228789

Historic Interiors: Oberstown, Lusk, Co. Dublin.
T: (01) 8437174; E: killian@historicinteriors.net

Helen Turkington: 47 Dunville Avenue,
Ranelagh, Dublin 6. T: (01) 4125138;
E: info@helenturkington.com;
www.helenturkington.com

Fired Earth: 19 George's Street Lower, Dún
Laoghaire, Co. Dublin. T: (01) 6636160;
www.firedearth.com

Lulabelle Design and Hire: 99 George's Street Upper,
Dún Laoghaire, Co. Dublin. T: (083) 1075633

Rubanesque: 59 William Street South, Dublin 2.
T: (01) 6729243; E: ribbons@arubanesque.ie;
www.arubanesque.ie

This book is typeset in Linux Libertine and Burford.

*The paper used in this book comes from the wood pulp
of managed forests. For every tree felled, at least one
tree is planted, thereby renewing natural resources.*

All rights reserved.
No part of this publication may be copied,
reproduced or transmitted in any form or by any
means, without written permission of the publishers.

A CIP catalogue record for this book is available from
the British Library.

To Ghinlon, Sean, Aislinn, Federica, Sicora, Tristan and Odhran

Vi voglio tanto tanto bene – Mam Eileen, Nonna Eileen

Grazie infinite and endless thanks to:

Two wonderful ladies, Orla Neligan and Joanne Murphy, for making my humble dishes look marvellous.

Joanna Twamley and Valentina Cipriani for trying out my recipes, much to the detriment of their waistlines!

Gianmarco Raimondo, the calmest chef I know – are you a Buddhist by any chance? Your unique smile and demeanour made our chore of creating the dishes for the photos a true pleasure.

The diligent Andrea Daniele for correcting my Italian spelling. I will never get to grips with those vowels at the end of words – is it *i*, *e*, *o* or *a*?

Deirdre Nolan of Gill & Macmillan, encouraging, guiding and reassuring.

Kristin Jensen, a gem of an editor, patient and passionate about food, thank you for bringing me back to the basics.

Fidelma Slattery, *grazia* for such a stylish and beautiful book.

Catherine Gough, whose emails brightened up my hectic days, jumping from one restaurant to another.

I owe special gratitude to Davide Izzo for being so supportive and for trusting my food ethos in our business.

What can I say to my husband, the steadfast Mr Stefano Crescenzi? Life has taken us on a most unexpected journey. I thought I would spend the rest of my life in Italy when I met you, yet here we are in Ireland, the last place you ever imagined living in. We abandoned good pensionable jobs for a leap into the unknown and discovered the magical world of restaurants. Who knows what awaits us?

To my children Ghinlon, Aislinn, Federica and Sean. I have so many fond memories of you all growing up in our restaurants – Federica and Aislinn, mere toddlers, hiding in the kitchen eating biscotti; Ghinlon juggling his schoolwork with working alongside us in setting up our first restaurant, very much the man of the house; and Sean as a young teenager working with the chefs, giving them advice! It has been a roller coaster for all of us. We have rowed and laughed along the way, and who knows just how many feasts we have shared – thousands. Now that you are all educated and have left home, I can finally buy myself that vintage Jaguar!

CONTENTS

Introduction · 1
Tricks of the trade · 14
Cooking no nos · 16
Where to buy Italian ingredients · 19

....

New Year's Eve Midnight Feast

Cenone di Capodanno

· 21 ·

....

Epiphany Lunch

Il Pranzo della Befana

· 31 ·

....

Midnight Feasts for Football and Politics

Cene di Mezzonotte

· 45 ·

....

Carnevale Late Afternoon Buffet Lunch in Masquerade

Un Buffet per Carnevale in Maschera

· 59 ·

....

A Romantic Dinner for St Valentine's Day

Una Cena Romantica per San Valentino

· 81 ·

Women's Day Mimosa Dinner
La Festa della Donna
· 95 ·

....

Father's Day
La Festa del Papá
· 111 ·

....

Easter Sunday and Monday Lunch
Il Pranzo di Pasqua e Pasquetta
· 129 ·

....

Mother's Day
La Festa della Mamma
· 143 ·

....

Labour Day Picnic
Primo Maggio
· 161 ·

....

Religious Festivities
Festivà Religiose
· 177 ·

....

Birthday and Names Day Dinner
Compleanno e Onomastico
· 195 ·

....

Mid-August Holiday Lunch
Ferragosto
· 209 ·

Sacred Sagre – Street Food
Le Sagre del Territorio

· 225 ·

....

October Truffle Celebrations
Sagra del Tartufo

· 239 ·

....

All Saints and Souls Days
Tutti i Santi e il Giorno dei Morti

· 247 ·

....

Ski Supper
Spuntino Serale Dopo lo Sci

· 263 ·

....

Christmas Eve Dinner
La Vigilia di Natale

· 271 ·

....

Christmas Day
Il Giorno di Natale

· 291 ·

....

St Stephen's Day (Boxing Day)
Il Giorno di Santo Stefano

· 305 ·

....

Index

· 320 ·

ITALIAN cuisine is a cultural and social art form that has developed over hundreds of years, revered by most and misrepresented by many. In this book I have portrayed my life in Italy through the culture of food.

I abandoned a culture with the belief that the family who prays together stays together and enthusiastically adopted one that believes the family who eats together stays together. In Italy, eating translates into saporous feasts, merriment and chat, and all guilt free. I had travelled from purgatory to heaven.

I have grown to love the Italian culture. And yet, in response to my almost daily outbursts eulogising everything Italian, a regular and impeccably dressed customer, supporter and precious critic of our Dunne & Crescenzi restaurant, the honourable Mr Stanford Kingston, tends to stop me in my tracks: 'Eileen, you are not Italian. Can I just remind you of that?'

Leabharlanna Poibli Chathair Baile Átha Cliath

Dublin City Public Libraries

How I ended up in Italy

It all started with one of my mother's youngest sisters, who was both brilliant and bold. I can still hear my grandmother saying in her smoky, husky voice, 'She's too smart for her own good.' She procured herself a good position with the UN in Rome and shortly afterwards my grandfather remarried. My remaining unmarried aunts weren't happy sharing the house with the new arrival, so off they went to Rome too. When I finished secondary school the threesome, who were always looking out for me, being the eldest niece, suggested I apply to art college in Rome. That done, I joined the newfound Irish colony and was properly pampered. Jean weaned me onto Italian food, Pauline taught me how to maintain a house and dress fittingly and Sheila schooled me in Italian culture. It was the taming of Eliza Doolittle *all' Italiana*. Needless to say, my sisters came too, followed by nieces, neighbours and friends – but no men!

Una bella tavola – a lovely table

When I think of Italian food, the first thing that comes to mind is setting the table. It is a ritual carried out with great attention in all Italian homes. The table must be properly set for every meal, whether it's breakfast, lunch or dinner, and this applies irrespective of a person's economic position. A well-set table conveys the feeling that all is well with the world. I have the sweetest memories of my daughter Aislinn subscribing to this philosophy when she was about two years of age. Accustomed to the routine at her crèche, every Saturday and Sunday precisely at midday, I would find her waiting patiently at the table, having carefully arranged her tablemat and napkin for lunch.

Every evening, the Italian table is set with a nice crisp tablecloth upon which is set the delph, cutlery, wine glasses, water glasses and napkins. Baskets of fresh bread, jugs of water and carafes of wine take centre stage. On special occasions, including Sundays, the best tablecloths are brought out, along with more elaborate delph, glasses and candelabra, creating an ostentatious table that marks that day as distinct. '*Tutti a tavola*' (everyone to the table) is the invitation to come take your place.

Tablecloths are part of a family's DNA and are passed down from generation to generation, washed, starched and ironed with true love and care. Tablecloths are not simply bought in a shop. Lengths of fabric are carefully chosen for design, quality and function (everyday or special occasion), a task that might involve a number of family members. After this the lace is selected and expertly matched to the fabric. Then both are sent off to the *sarta* (tailor) to have the tablecloth made up.

Our family buys the fabric from a beautiful, tiny, traditional shop, Buschi in Grottazzolina in the Marche, which has stunning views out over the Sibillini Hills. Mr Buschi, against the backdrop of a severe black and white portrait of his father, the founder of the shop, rolls out huge bolts of fabric on his ancient wooden counter. After much deliberation, when we have chosen our favourites, he takes an enormous scissors and cuts through the fabric with an engineer's precision. Now it's time to choose the lace. Mr Buschi unfurls great big balls of cotton lace and latticed lace on the counter and the deliberations start all over again. Should it be wide or narrow, simple or intricate, beige, white or pastel? Mr Buschi is consulted at great length and gladly lends a hand in making the final decisions.

Finally, the chosen fabrics and lace are parcelled together and sent to *carissima* Anna, the town *sarta*. Mr Buschi will eventually post them to Ireland, and it's so exhilarating to receive those lovely brown paper parcels tied with twine, showcasing Mr Buschi's particular handwriting. Mr Buschi calls us every Christmas Eve to send us his best wishes. He is now in his eighties and lately I have come across him smoking two cigarettes at a time.

When my husband Stefano's grandmother, Nonna Valentina, was alive, she painstakingly embroidered elaborate tablecloths for all of her children and grandchildren and crocheted fine cotton lace trim with the tiniest well-worn crochet hook. Each design was selected with that child or grandchild in mind. She undertook this work each evening after dinner while she watched her favourite chat shows on TV, finished crosswords, munched on forbidden caramels hidden in her multi-pocketed apron and talked incessantly. So now you can understand when I say that tablecloths are part of a family's heritage.

Una bella sala da pranzo – a beautiful dining room

Eating together is a daily ritual in Italy. It's a time to come together to share food and thoughts and to make sure everybody is cared for. It's not surprising, therefore, that dining rooms and dining spaces are an important part of Italian homes. Farmhouses tend to have two huge kitchens incorporating expansive dining areas specifically to house enormous dining tables. The farmhouse kitchen is the soul of the home and is situated in the main part of the house. This is where the family gather to prepare their daily food, eat all of their meals and spend valuable time with friends and each other. The second kitchen is situated at garden level, perhaps in a converted garage, to facilitate al fresco dining. This space is also used to make and store homemade sauces and preserves and is the beating heart of the *vendemmia* (grape harvest). Family and workers will dine here together and stories will be told and retold about harvests gone by. However, most Italians live in apartments and you may be surprised to learn that their kitchens are actually quite modest, with a very small table neatly tucked away in a corner used solely for breakfast. Culinary miracles occur in these small kitchens, but Italians are wonderfully creative in managing space and packing everything away efficiently.

They are also natural 'dining curators'. Dining spaces in the home are meticulously curated. Paintings are hung on the wall to provide good conversation topics, while a nice cupboard housing lovely tableware, a liquor and wine unit and distinct overhead lighting never fail to impress. In some homes I have visited, the family warmly crowd into the kitchen for everyday meals while Sunday lunches and special occasions are served in the dining room. Here, the dining chairs still maintain their original plastic covering, a heavy-legged table is draped with a thick protective covering, family heirlooms bleakly dress the walls and dim chandeliers forlornly droop from the ceiling. That all changes when the room fills with chatter, the aroma of great food and the clinking of glasses, and those heirlooms start to talk back.

Feste Italiane (Italian feasts)

I encourage you to create warm and memorable dining experiences simply by fashioning a beautiful or bohemian table. Surprise your guests with food nestling in parchment paper tied up with colourful ribbons. Use mismatching dishes, boards and baskets, particularly ones you are fond of and ones that have a story: 'this was my grandmother's' or 'I picked up these forks at a market stall when I was in Umbria'. Most of all, I hope you will find hosting dinners for groups of friends and family fun and that each affair becomes a memorable *festa*. Besides the established feast days and birthdays, any occasion is a good opportunity to create conviviality, whether it's football and rugby matches, promotions, pre-exams, post-exams, pre-vacations, returns from vacations, catching-up dinners or homecomings, and please have a Women's Day dinner.

Cooking for large groups doesn't need to be cumbersome. Try serving smaller amounts of several different plates to be shared. And cooking can be communal, where everyone brings a dish to the table. In Italy, large serving plates are placed in the middle of the table. The host will portion out the first round of food but then everyone helps themselves to seconds. You are free to eat as little or as much as you wish, but a good Italian host will make sure you eat much more than you intended.

What I want you to get from this book is your new signature dish, the one that everyone asks you to bring to their dinners: 'Joseph is bringing his brilliant stuffed tomatoes'; 'Sadbh is bringing her amazing porcini mushroom lasagne.' Your dish becomes the icebreaker and everyone will want your recipe.

The menus I have put together are deliberately eclectic in order to offer you a little taste of the varied Italian kitchen, from the pistachio groves of Sicily to the *rifugi* (mountain retreats) of the Dolomites. Every occasion can be a cause for celebration. Celebrating even the very simplest foods is emblematic of Italians' respect for nature, for people and for life itself. *Buon appetito, amici miei.*

TRICKS *of the* TRADE

BACK TO BASICS

The basis of most Italian dishes is a *soffritto*: finely chopped onion, carrot and celery; garlic and chilli; or simply a finely sliced onion. *Soffritto* is used to start off a stew, casserole, braised meats and meat-based pasta sauces. Garlic and chilli are used to start fish-based pasta sauces, pan-fried vegetables known as *ripassata in padella* and *arrabbiata* pasta sauces. Finely sliced onion is used for risottos and *sugo al pomodoro* (simple tomato sauce).

A LITTLE WATER GOES A LONG WAY

Always retain half a cup of water from the pot the pasta is cooking in. If you find that the final dish is too dry when you mix the pasta with the sauce, add a little of the cooking water. This is particularly useful for fish-based pasta dishes.

Pasta sauces tend to dry up, so thin them with a little water from the pasta cooking pot. Nonna Valentina, Stefano's grandmother, always told me '*allungare, allungare*' (lengthen, lengthen). She maintained my sauces were too thick.

A LITTLE SAUCE GOES A LONG WAY TOO

Italian pasta dishes don't require huge amounts of sauce. One 400g tin of cherry or plum tomatoes makes enough sauce for 500g pasta (enough for five or six people). Take a *ragù*, for instance. One tin of tomatoes and 250g of minced meat is sufficient, while an *amatriciana* would require no more than 100g of pancetta or guanciale. There is no need to pile in the meat or the bacon.

ZIO ALBERTO'S SECRET

We all love sprinkling freshly grated parmigiano or Pecorino on our pasta dishes, particularly those with a tomato-based sauce, but Stefano's Uncle Alberto drains the pasta, mixes the pasta with the grated cheese and then adds the sauce. He maintains it's much tastier and I have to agree.

DRIED CHILLI FLAKES

I tend to use dried chilli flakes, but you could use some fresh red chilli instead. I like the unique flavour of dried Calabrian chilli flakes, but I also use them because that way you don't run the watery-eyed risk of biting on a very hot chilli.

LEAVE TO REST

One of Nonna Valentina's culinary chants was *lascia riposare* (leave to rest). While this may sound strange, it makes sense. When you cook a *stracotto* (braised meat), it needs to rest for 10 minutes before slicing. Sponge cakes should rest in the baking tin, as they will be easier to remove after 10 minutes of resting. Even meatballs will taste better for taking a *riposino* (little rest).

COOKING

— No Nos —

Dried basil

The taste of dried basil is very different from fresh basil. If you don't have fresh basil, just leave it out of a recipe altogether.

Tomato paste

Tomato paste doesn't resemble tomatoes in form or in taste. It adds a dull colour and sour taste to your dish and is best left out of any recipe. Chop a couple of fresh tomatoes or use some tinned tomatoes instead.

Garlic-infused oil

Every now and then I come across chefs using garlic-infused oil in our restaurant kitchens and I promptly bin it. If you use garlic-infused oil, everything has the same overpowering, oily garlic taste.

Browned minced meat

When preparing a *ragù*, the meat should be stirred in the oil until it takes on a nice deep colour, not until it becomes dark brown and dry and separates into meat crumbs.

Layers of béchamel in a lasagne

Béchamel sauce should be drizzled lightly over each layer, not plastered on one or even two inches thick.

Mushy pasta

Al dente seems to mean different things to different people, and I like my pasta cooked really al dente. I suggest you cook dried pasta for one minute less than the time indicated on the packet and cook fresh pasta for a couple of minutes only, testing it every now and then. Don't do your wonderful sauce that you have spent a lot of time preparing an injustice by serving it with overcooked pasta.

Mushy risotto

We all talk about al dente pasta, but risotto should have a bite too. All too often I come across mushy risotto that is more akin to a savoury rice pudding. I mostly use Carnaroli rice when making risotto because it has a good starch content and retains a bite. Vialone Nano rice is best for soupy risottos. I don't like Arborio rice because it tends to be lumpy, but it's the variety that is most widely available. No matter which kind of rice you use, risotto requires patience for the best results.

Over-ripe tomatoes

You need nice, firm, ripe tomatoes for a salad or a *bruschetta al pomodoro*. If your tomatoes have softened, make an alternative *bruschetta*: caramelise them in a little olive oil with one clove of garlic and serve on toasted ciabatta.

Smothering everything in cream

I like to taste individual ingredients in a dish, but too much cream can smother their identity. Use cream sparingly – just a hint is good.

Olive oil

Italian families stock up on a year's supply of olive oil just before Christmas; many families even have a favourite mill that they buy their oil from. It's a lovely tradition and better than buying supermarket oil, which is often a blend of oils from several countries. Everyone talks about olive oil at Christmastime. You overhear conversations on the bus, in the grocery shop and at the hairdresser about a relative somewhere in Puglia, Calabria, Sicily, Tuscany, Umbria or Liguria ready to dispense this culinary gold.

All olives are green, and olive oil extracted from an early harvest of green olives is the best. Olives turn black towards the end of their natural life on the trees, when it's easier to harvest them. But black olives don't necessarily give the best oil. Harvesting green olives is labour intensive, as the olives are hand picked and crushed within 24 hours. Understandably, this type of olive oil can be very expensive. In Italy, the good oil is kept for salads and dressings.

The reasonably priced olive oil sitting on our supermarket shelves mostly comes from black olives that have been accumulated into huge mountains, and they can be waiting quite a while to be processed. Even though it might say 'extra virgin olive oil' on the label, there is more than meets the eye: these oils are highly processed, deodorised and full of additives. I believe that sometimes you are better off using a good block of butter instead of cheap olive oil that tastes like paint stripper and does nothing for your cooking.

Garlicky *bruschetta*

Bread toasted with masses of garlic and oil is just plain yucky. There is nothing as nice as taking a thick slice of country loaf, toasting it, rubbing a little garlic on one side, drizzling it with extra virgin olive oil and sprinkling with salt.

Overloading

Most Italian dishes are made from a couple of ingredients that marry well together. Don't think you have to put every Italian ingredient you have ever heard of into every Italian dish you prepare.

Stereotypical vegetarian dishes

Italian cuisine is ideal for vegetarians. It's based on an abundance of diverse vegetables that form the backbone of the Mediterranean kitchen. A good lasagna for vegetarians, made with porcini mushrooms, pesto or artichokes, can be found on menus throughout Italy. They are nothing like the 'vegetarian lasagna' you see so often here, laden down with peppers, aubergines, courgettes, onions, herbs and nuts. That is too many ingredients to make a good marriage. Simplicity is key.

Where to buy Italian ingredients

Most of the ingredients mentioned in this book are available from good
supermarkets. If you have difficulty finding an unusual product or want to source
good-quality ingredients, try these stores or consult the McKennas' Irish Food Guide
or Georgina Campbell's Ireland Guide for a good deli or shop near you.

....

Ardkeen Quality Food Store, Dunmore Road, Waterford

Avoca, Rathcoole, Co. Dublin

Best of Italy, Dunville Avenue, Ranelagh, Co. Dublin

Cavistons, 58 Glasthule Road, Sandycove, Co. Dublin

Country Choice, Nenagh, Co. Tipperary

Dunne & Crescenzi Casa, 17 South Frederick Street, Dublin 2

English Market, Cork City

Fallon & Byrne, 11 Exchequer Street, Dublin 2

Gleeson's Food Store, Roscommon

La Corte, Epicurean Food Court, Abbey Street, Dublin 1

McCambridges, 38 Shop Street, Galway City

Olive Delicatessen, Skerries, Co. Dublin

Sawers, Fountain Centre, College Street, Belfast

Sheridans, 11 South Anne Street, Dublin 2

Sheridans, Church Yard Station, Galway City

Sheridans, Virginia Road Station, Kells, Co. Meath

Swanton's, 639 Lisburn Road, Belfast

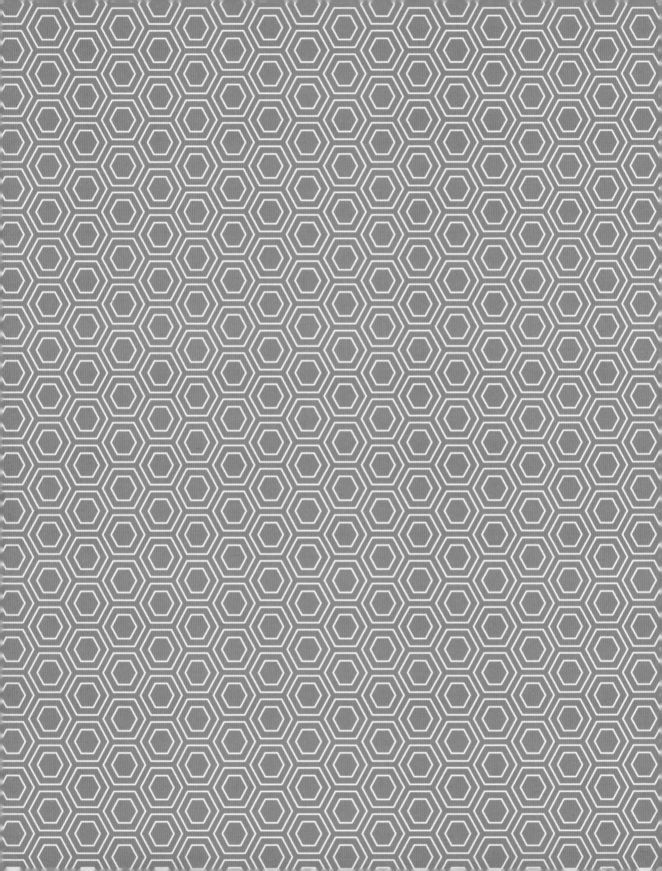

NEW YEAR'S EVE MIDNIGHT FEAST

Cenone di Capodanno

PRESENT

Family, friends and neighbours

....

SOUP

Lentil soup with Colonnata lardo crostini

MAINS

Lentils and sausages

DESSERT

Cantuccini biscuits with cranberries and chocolate

THROW out the old and bring in the new. It's midnight in Naples and locals throw anything and everything from their windows down onto the streets below – plates, glasses, even old TVs. It's advisable to steer clear of those inviting, meandering side streets and take refuge in the wide open spaces of Piazza del Plebiscito. This tradition continues only in some populist suburbs of Rome now that the inhabitants of the *centro storico* have been ousted by bourgeois speculators.

Back in 1980, I felt my newborn son, Ghinlon, deserved a better and safer mode of transport than travelling around strapped to me as I veered in and out of chaotic traffic on my very old Ciao *motorino*. Having saved conscientiously, a used Fiat 128 was purchased, revealing the imprints and dents of 10 previous owners. On the morning of the first of the year, following an intense night of neighbourhood celebrations, I was dismayed to find a washing machine sitting on top of my relatively new acquisition. Attempts to squeeze behind the wheel beneath the fallen roof lining were made in vain and, needless to say, the car was a write-off. I took it in my stride. After all, there is a price to be paid if you want to live in a particularly unique culture. Now where was that reliable old *motorino*?

New Year's Eve in Italy tends to be a great family-and-friends affair involving a late, elaborate and extensive dinner similar to Christmas

Eve. The countdown to midnight is all-important and the lead-up to it is consumed with playing card games. Substantial amounts of money have been spent on illegal fireworks and every balcony, courtyard and terrace hosts elaborate displays, a feast for the heart and eyes. There's no singing, I'm afraid, but plenty of spumante. The sound of fireworks mingling with the popping corks of bottles of bubbly is reminiscent of Verdi's 'Triumphal March'. Midnight calls for lentils, as the general belief has it that eating lentils will ensure an adequate supply of money throughout the following year.

Another tradition involves red lingerie. The ladies of the house or *festa* all disappear into a bedroom just before midnight and change into red lingerie, evoking fertility. The windows of high street shops showcase tantalising red lingerie during the week between Christmas and New Year.

Restaurants bump up their prices significantly on New Year's Eve and are best avoided, as the atmosphere tends to be cold and the staff don't want to be there. An alternative option would be to gate crash a family affair or simply picnic in a central piazza, where there is bound to be a great buzz and amazing fireworks.

Lentil soup with Colonnata lardo crostini

Zuppa di lenticchie con toast di lardo di Colonnata

Melt-in-the-mouth Tuscan lardo di Colonnata or lardo di Arnard from Val d'Aosta are akin to elegant butter, nothing like the thick, greasy lard we might be familiar with. I always remember what Stefano's grandmother, Nonna Valentina, used to say: '*Un pò di tutto ma con moderazione*' (a little of everything in moderation). She lived to be 99 and she loved her lard, butter and salumi. However, I think she said this more as a justification for indulging in her favourite treats.

PLACE THE LENTILS, onions, carrots and celery in a large saucepan of salted cold water. Bring to the boil, then reduce the heat to low and simmer for 45 minutes to 1 hour, until the lentils are soft. Add some warm water if the lentils look too dry. When the lentils are done, remove the vegetables and mash them with a fork.

Heat the olive oil in a large saucepan over a low heat. Sauté the garlic for about 1 minute, just until it's fragrant but not browned, then stir in the chilli flakes and vegetable mash and pour in the red wine. Increase the heat momentarily to cook off the alcohol, then reduce the heat again. Add the tomato passata and allow it to heat through, then add the lentils. Pour everything into a blender and blend to a creamy consistency. Return to the pan to heat through.

Toast the ciabatta slices and place a slice of lard on top while the toast is very hot. Ladle the soup into 12 small soup bowls and place a piece of lard toast in each one.

SERVES 12

1kg lentils from Castelluccio or Colfiorito (or Puy lentils)
2 medium onions, peeled
2 medium carrots, scrubbed
2 sticks of celery
8 tablespoons extra virgin olive oil
4 garlic cloves, crushed
1 tablespoon dried chilli flakes
150ml red wine
150ml tomato passata
1 ciabatta, cut into 12 slices
250g wafer-thin slices of Colonnata lard

Lentils and sausages

Lenticchie con salsiccia

Although cotechino, a type of fat sausage emulating a pig's trotter, is traditionally eaten with lentils on New Year's Eve, try lentils with fresh Italian sausage, known as salsiccia.

PLACE THE LENTILS, sausages, onions, carrots and celery in a large saucepan of salted cold water. Bring to the boil, then reduce the heat to low and simmer for 45 minutes to 1 hour, until the lentils are soft. Add some warm water if the lentils look too dry. When the lentils are done, remove the vegetables and mash them with a fork.

Heat the olive oil in a large saucepan or wok over a low heat. Sauté the garlic for about 1 minute, just until it's fragrant but not browned, then stir in the chilli flakes and vegetable mash and pour in the red wine. Increase the heat momentarily to cook off the alcohol, then reduce the heat again. Add the tomato passata and allow it to heat through, then add the lentils and sausages. Simmer for 5 minutes, then remove from the heat.

Serve big ladles of the sausage and lentils with toasted bread drizzled with extra virgin olive oil. Sprinkle with chopped fresh parsley.

SERVES 10–12

1kg lentils from Castelluccio or Colfiorito (or Puy lentils)
6 fresh Italian salsiccia sausages, cut in half
2 medium onions, peeled
2 medium carrots, scrubbed
2 sticks of celery
8 tablespoons extra virgin olive oil
4 garlic cloves
1 tablespoon dried chilli flakes
150ml red wine
150ml tomato passata
bunch of fresh flat-leaf parsley, chopped

Small lentils give the best results. The tiny Castellucio and Colfiorito varieties are my absolute favourites.

Cantuccini biscuits with cranberries and chocolate

Cantuccini con mirtilli rossi e cioccolata

Traditional almond *cantuccini* are dipped in dessert wine, such as Tuscan vin santo, and offered as an alternative to dessert at the end of a meal. These *cantuccini* with cranberries and chocolate tend to be softer and are suited to freshly brewed tea and coffee.

One morning, Nonna Valentina was horrified to discover me making tea for her grandson in her grand kitchen in Torino. '*Sciacqua budelle* (intestines rinse),' she muttered. 'My grandson only drinks coffee in the morning.' And thus I was temporarily barred from the kitchen.

PREHEAT THE OVEN to 150℃. Grease a large baking tray.

Mix the flour, sugar and baking powder together in a large bowl. Moisten with the beaten eggs, then add the dried cranberries, chocolate chips and orange zest.

Turn the dough out onto a lightly floured work surface and roll into a thick log. Cut in half to form two logs that are each about 5cm in diameter and 30cm long. Place on the greased tray and bake for 20 minutes.

Remove and cool on a wire rack for about 15 minutes, until the logs are cool enough to handle. Slice into 2cm-thick biscuits and place on the tray cut side up. Return to the oven for another 15 minutes. Spread out on a wire rack to cool completely before storing in an airtight container.

MAKES 25 BISCUITS

200g plain flour

150g caster sugar

1 level teaspoon baking powder

2 free-range or organic eggs, beaten

100g dried cranberries

100g dark chocolate chips

zest of ½ orange

The very best almond cantuccini *are made by Maria at the Da Maria* trattoria *in Capalbio and the recipe is in my previous book. This lovely* trattoria *offering local Tuscan food is well worth the detour if you are in the vicinity of Porto Santo Stefano or heading from Rome to Florence (or vice versa).*

EPIPHANY LUNCH

Il Pranzo della Befana

PRESENT

Family, special friends and little ones

....

ANTIPASTO

Braised Romanesco artichokes

PASTA

Pennette with mussels, aubergines and whipped ricotta

MAINS

Pork escalopes with a pistachio crust

SIDES

Red cabbage and Teroldego wine

DESSERT

Limoncello rice pudding cake

YOU have just recovered from three or four days of Christmas feasting, refereed umpteen political scraps, managed to avoid being rude when being questioned (i.e. criticised) incessantly about how non-Italians rear their children and survived the potential effects of gluttony and avarice when you are called back by the *famiglia* for the Epiphany lunch.

As a *straniera* (foreigner), this takes some getting used to, especially a free-spirited *straniera* who has left her home country, has shunned family ties to some extent, is fiercely independent and doesn't like being told when and when not to eat. But the initial reluctance instantly fades when greeted with the aroma of braised artichokes emanating from the in-laws' kitchen, Nonna's warm, robust hugs and the happiness radiating from the children from being around their *nonni* and *zii* (grandparents and aunts), and you are overwhelmed with guilt.

After lunch, when the children are being spoiled with toys and the traditional sweet coals from the *Befana*, it's time for Stefano and I to make our escape to Piazza Navona for a hot chocolate and roast chestnuts and to browse the stalls of sticky sweets, fairground games and pretty *presepe*.

Braised Romanesco artichokes

Carciofi alla romana

Artichokes are an integral part of the Jewish Roman culinary experience. Il Pompiere restaurant in the Ghetto area behind the synagogue serves up the best pasta dishes with artichokes you will ever have the privilege of eating. I adore their antipasti and *primi* pasta dishes. Sit back and soak up the *Felliniana* atmosphere in the restaurant.

When you live in Italy, it's essential to form an alliance with your vegetable vendor, who probably runs a little stall in the local daily market. It is through your loyalty to your vendor that you can expect the best and freshest fruit and veg, because the last thing you want are woody artichokes. You will be furnished with the sweetest plums, the juiciest, fattest cherries, luscious figs and honeyed apricots. You can also place your order in advance and have the vendor do most of the prep work for you, leaving you with ready-to-cook artichokes, topped and tailed French beans, chopped mixed leaves for salads and prepared vegetable mixes for minestrone.

POUND THE GARLIC, parsley, mint and salt together in a pestle and mortar and set aside.

Remove the tough outer leaves from the artichokes (the more the merrier) and scoop out the furry beards from the centre. Using a sharp knife, cut at least 2.5cm off the top of the artichoke and cut off the jagged edges. Cut and scrape the stalks to about 3cm in length.

Continued overleaf

SERVES 12

6 garlic cloves, peeled and left whole
good bunch of fresh flat-leaf parsley, finely chopped
good bunch of fresh mint, finely chopped (reserve some leaves as garnish)
1 level teaspoon salt
12 medium Romanesco artichokes
2 lemons
12 tablespoons extra virgin olive oil
150ml dry white wine
150ml warm water

Cut the lemons in half. Holding half a lemon in one hand and an artichoke in the other hand, rub each artichoke with the lemon. Open the leaves of the artichokes and stuff with the garlic and herb paste.

Warm the olive oil in a wide, heavy-based saucepan over a low heat. Place the artichokes in the pan head down. (You may need to divide the batch between two saucepans.) Sauté for a couple of minutes, then add the wine and cook for a few minutes more. Add the warm water, cover and cook over a low heat for 30 minutes, until the artichokes are tender. Add a little extra warm water if they look like they're too dry. When they are ready, you should be able to easily cut through the artichokes with a knife.

Serve one artichoke per person. Drizzle over the juices from the saucepan and garnish with some fresh mint leaves.

There is a bit of work involved in preparing artichokes, so it's best to go ahead and prepare a good amount. Use them for antipasti, pasta dishes, sides or mains for vegetarian friends.

Pennette with mussels, aubergines and whipped ricotta

Pennette con cozze, melanzane e ricotta montata

When I travel to cities such as London or New York, it's so inspiring to encounter truly innovative Italian food served in modern eateries. The amazing Rose Gray and Ruth Rogers of the iconic River Café in London set the standard back in the 1990s with their fresh approach to Italian cooking, and others continue to make strides.

I believe this innovation is being transferred back to Italy. Over the last 10 years or so, I have observed young Italian chefs offering a fresher and more interesting style of Italian cooking. Isn't that what Italian cooking is all about – an influx of influences? I often overhear Stefano mentoring young chefs and imparting his respect of traditional cooking methods. He believes you can only be innovative once you have understood the fundamentals of traditional cooking.

During a trip to Boston I encountered the wonderfully talented, dynamic chef Lidia Shire. Lidia uses whipped ricotta a lot in her cooking at her fantastic Scampo restaurant. It adds depth and richness to finish off otherwise simple dishes.

RINSE THE MUSSELS in cold water and pull off the beards. Tap any open mussels on the side of a plate or the counter, and if they don't close, discard them. Steep in plenty of cold water for at least 1 hour and change the water several times.

Continued overleaf

SERVES 6

1kg fresh mussels

500g ridged pennette pasta

8 tablespoons extra virgin olive oil

2 aubergines, diced into 2cm cubes

2 garlic cloves, peeled and left whole

1 teaspoon dried chilli flakes

100ml white wine

150g ricotta

zest of 1 lemon

1 tablespoon finely chopped fresh flat-leaf parsley

salt

Cook the pasta in a large saucepan of boiling salted water until al dente or according to the instructions on the packet.

Heat 4 tablespoons of olive oil in a large saucepan over a medium heat. Add the diced aubergines, cover the pan and cook for 10 minutes, stirring regularly.

In a separate large saucepan (one that is big enough to also take all the pasta later), heat the remaining 4 tablespoons of olive oil over a low heat. Sauté the garlic for about 1 minute, just until it's fragrant but not browned. Add the chilli flakes, mussels and white wine. Cover and cook until all of the mussels have opened. Discard any unopened mussels.

Whip the ricotta for 30 seconds in a blender with the lemon zest and parsley.

Drain the pasta and add to the saucepan of mussels. Add the aubergines, season with salt to taste and mix well.

Divide the pasta between six pasta bowls. Top each portion with a dollop of whipped ricotta.

You can remove the mussels from the shells before mixing them with the pasta if you wish. Otherwise, put a big bowl on the table for the empty shells.

Pork escalopes with a pistachio crust

Scaloppine di maiale in crosta di pistacchio

Should you happen to visit Catania in Sicily towards the end of September or the beginning of October, make a point of visiting the pistachio festival in the town of Bronte near Mount Etna. Hand picking pistachio nuts from the trees that sprout amongst the hard lava rocks is sheer hard work. These brilliant green nuts are an enviable ingredient for desserts and savoury dishes. They are used extensively in Sicilian cuisine and are referred to locally as green gold. The Bronte variety is particularly sought after because of its fragrant and aromatic flavour and wonderful, intense colour. You will no doubt be offered a palette of traditional nibbles as you wander amongst the stalls of delight at the *Sagra del Pistacchio* in the town.

USING A PESTLE AND MORTAR, pound together the crushed pistachios, parsley and some salt and pepper before working in the 150ml of olive oil.

Coat the pork pieces on one side with the pistachio mix. Place on a plate or baking tray, cover loosely with cling film and leave in the fridge for 2 hours.

Preheat the oven to 200°C.

Heat a little olive oil in a low-rimmed casserole dish over a low heat. Sweat the garlic in the oil for about 1 minute, just until the garlic is fragrant but not browned. Remove the garlic with a slotted spoon and discard. Add the pork to the dish, coated side up, and let it sizzle for a minute. Pour in the wine and increase the heat momentarily to cook off the alcohol.

Place the dish in the oven and roast for 10 minutes, until the meat is firm to the touch and the crust is nicely toasted (or if you have a meat thermometer, it should read 160–170°C). Serve with the red cabbage on page 41.

SERVES 10

300g pistachio nuts, shelled and crushed

1 tablespoon chopped fresh flat-leaf parsley

salt and freshly ground black pepper

150ml extra virgin olive oil, plus extra for frying

2 whole free-range pork fillets, cut into 20 x 3cm-thick circles

2 garlic cloves, peeled and left whole

150ml dry white wine

Hazelnuts can be used instead of pistachios.

Red cabbage and Teroldego wine

Cavolo rosso al Teroldego

Northern Italy is not blessed with the flavoursome tomatoes, aubergines and peppers of the south, but red cabbage cooked in the local Teroldego wine can be just as memorable. Elisabetta Foradori, an unrivalled Teroldego producer, is always pushing the boundaries, such as producing biodynamic wines. I don't necessarily seek out organic wines, but I have to say that Elisabetta's wines are outstanding and they deserve the plaudits she receives. In this recipe, the magnificent deep purple juices of the cabbage are reflected in the wine.

HEAT THE OLIVE OIL in a large saucepan over a medium heat. Sauté the onion for about 5 minutes, until softened. Add the cabbage and cook for 2 minutes more. Pour in the wine and increase the heat momentarily to cook off the alcohol.

Cover and cook for 45 minutes over a low heat, until the cabbage is soft and tender. Add a little warm water if it looks too dry. Season with salt to taste.

SERVES 6

4 tablespoons extra virgin olive oil
1 medium onion, diced
1 head of red cabbage, shredded
½ bottle of Teroldego or another full-bodied red wine
salt

Red cabbage is very good with most pork dishes, including the venerable sausage.

Limoncello rice pudding cake

Budino di riso con limoncello

If you visit Verona, book a show at the Arena di Verona and treat yourself to an open-air opera in this captivating ancient Roman amphitheatre. Indulge in traditional Veronese cuisine and enjoy fragrant, golden *budini* in Piazza delle Erbe sitting alongside the Fountain Madonna Verona. *Questa si che é vita –* that's the life!

TO MAKE THE PASTRY, cream the butter, sugar and lemon zest together until pale and fluffy. Add in the egg and mix well. Mix in the flour, then turn out onto a lightly floured board and knead lightly to form a soft dough. Wrap in cling film and place in the fridge for at least 2 hours.

To make the filling, pour the milk and water into a saucepan. Add the rice and bring to a simmer, then lower the heat, cover and cook for 30 minutes, stirring regularly, until the rice is soft. Fold in the muscovado sugar and leave to cool a little.

When the rice is getting towards the end of its cooking time, preheat the oven to 180°C.

Roll out the pastry to line a 25cm fluted quiche tin. You can blind bake it if you like, but it's not really necessary (see the note).

Add the beaten eggs, lemon zest and limoncello to the rice and mix lightly. Pour into the pastry-lined baking tin, leaving a 0.5cm border around the edge. Bake in the hot oven for about 30 minutes, until the pastry is golden and the filling is set. Leave to rest for 10 minutes before cutting. Sift the icing sugar over the pudding just before serving. Serve small helpings, as it's a filling dessert.

SERVES 8–10

For the pastry:
100g butter, softened
100g caster sugar
zest of ½ lemon
1 free-range or organic egg, beaten
200g plain flour

For the filling:
1 litre milk
250ml water
250g Carnaroli rice
150g dark or light brown muscovado sugar or granulated sugar
2 free-range or organic eggs, beaten
zest of 1 lemon
30ml limoncello di Sorrento
2 tablespoons icing sugar

I have given up on blind baking for casual dinners. Italians don't do blind baking, and your cake is most likely going to be eaten shortly after it comes out of the oven anyway.

MIDNIGHT FEASTS FOR FOOTBALL AND POLITICS

Cene di Mezzonotte

PRESENT

Friends and foes

....

ANTIPASTO

Baked crostini with mozzarella, prosciutto and figs

PASTA

Tomato and chilli penne

Spaghettata of garlic and chilli spaghetti

MAINS

Velvety vegetable soup with Altamura crostini

Zio Mario's eggs and peas

DESSERT

Ciambellini wine biscotti

MIDNIGHT suppers are popular in Italy, particularly during periods of political turmoil (which are often!) and major football events (which are equally as frequent). Long evenings of political debates or football drama invariably end with midnight suppers. Politics is a prominent conversational topic and initiation starts from a young age around the dining table, then progresses to the school *mensa* (cafeteria) and graduates to serious debates at university.

As a young student at l'Accademia di Belle Arti (College of Art) in Via di Ripetta in the mid-1970s, a number of us were locked in college for three days, under siege from ultra-right-wing fascist attacks. The enormous, ancient wooden doors were slammed shut with a deafening thud. Notwithstanding the serious political debates that took place around the clock, food was discussed at great lengths too. By the second day we were seriously hungry and tales of the best meals ever consumed were dished out like hallucinations. Being a streetwise Dublin girl, I volunteered to climb over a back wall, make my way home and prepare food. Ari, a young Greek student, offered to accompany me.

We prepared huge pots of *arrabbiata* pasta that we tied up with clothes (no fancy containers or cling film back in those days) and my Uncle Maurizio eagerly accompanied us back in my aunt's old Fiat 126. I suspect he was rekindling his own infamous 1968 student days. We somehow managed to scramble back over the rear wall and haul up the food. What a sight awaited us. Desks had been pushed together to form a huge medieval-like banquet table. A multitude of students' scarves were laid creatively to form a beautiful multicoloured tablecloth. Disposable plates and cutlery were majestically set out sitting on origami folded toilet paper. Dinner was served and we fed at least 50 extremely hungry students.

Everyone complained that the pasta was too spicy and I heard about their *zia* (aunt), *mamma* or *nonna* who did this and that with their *arrabbiata* sauce – the best anyone could dream of, of course. The suggestions continued well into the early hours. I will stop here and spare you the details of the ensuing relationships formed that night, but suffice it to say that my first marriage unfolded over those three days.

Baked crostini with mozzarella, prosciutto and figs

Crostini con mozzarella, prosciutto e fichi

In August, when the fig trees are laden down with fruits hidden amongst the huge leaves and fallen figs burst open to form a sweet nectared carpet at the base of the trees, it's time to pull out the fig recipes.

Baked crostini are a delicious starter, and creamy melted mozzarella, salty prosciutto and honeyed figs are a sublime combination.

PREHEAT THE OVEN to 200°C.

Brush a baking tray with olive oil and place the ciabatta slices on the tray. Top each piece of bread with a slice of mozzarella and ham.

Bake in the oven until the mozzarella softens, but don't allow it to melt completely. Remove from the oven and top each crostino with half a fig. Drizzle with olive oil and a little honey and eat immediately.

MAKES 12 CROSTINI

extra virgin olive oil

1 or 2 ciabatta or baguettes, cut into 12 slices 2cm thick

3 x 100g balls of mozzarella, each ball cut into 4 pieces

6 slices of prosciutto, each slice cut in half

6 figs, halved

2 tablespoons runny honey

The best figs are the small, late-season settembrini, *which are available in September.*

Tomato and chilli penne

Penne all'arrabbiata

Even though we run a number of restaurants, Stefano has always insisted on home-cooked family meals at least five days of the week. When our children were highly opinionated teenagers, I often thought of giving up on that philosophy. More often than not the meals ended in fiery debates due to diverging political ideologies, parenting methods that they didn't agree with (apparently we were unusually strict) or the menu that evening. Teenagers tend to experiment with food concepts, and ours could change from week to week.

In hindsight, it was worth it. Perhaps it has kept them close to each other and now whenever I ask where they would like to have their birthday dinners, the answer is always the same: a big family dinner, 'and don't forget to invite Alessandro, Granny, Auntie Pat, Laura and Claudio!' Those dinners seem to be getting bigger and bigger as more and more friends tag along.

COOK THE PASTA in a large saucepan of boiling salted water until al dente or according to the instructions on the packet.

Heat the oil in a wide saucepan over a low heat. Gently sauté the garlic for about 1 minute, just until it's fragrant – avoid browning the garlic at all costs. Stir in the chilli flakes, then add the tomatoes and salt to the pan.

Cover and cook for 10 minutes over a medium heat, stirring occasionally. Mash the tomatoes with the back of a wooden spoon to break them down a little more. If the sauce looks too dry, add a couple of spoons of cooking water from the pasta pot.

Drain the pasta and add it to the saucepan. Stir to coat with the sauce, sprinkle with the parsley and serve immediately.

SERVES 4–6

500g penne pasta

12 tablespoons extra virgin olive oil

4 garlic cloves, peeled and left whole

1 level teaspoon dried chilli flakes

1 x 400g tin of whole plum tomatoes

1 teaspoon salt

1 tablespoon finely chopped fresh flat-leaf parsley

Trattoria Danico at Piazza Vittorio in Rome makes a memorable *penne all'arrabbiata. This sauce also works well as a dip for fried fish.*

Spaghettata of garlic and chilli spaghetti

Spaghetti aglio, olio e peperoncino

I suppose *spaghettata* describes impromptu get togethers. At the mention of spaghetti, all hands rush on deck and an iconic pasta dish for ravenous revellers appears.

My good friend, the painter and sculptor Tonino Caporale, keeps me supplied with his addictive Calabrian chilli flake mixture. As young students hanging around the eateries of Via Ripetta, every meal was sprinkled with Tonino's precious chilli flakes, which he carried around in a sculptured snuffbox. This simple gesture was a constant reminder of home, his *terra* and his beloved Caterina.

COOK THE SPAGHETTI in a large saucepan of boiling salted water until al dente or according to the packet instructions.

When the pasta has almost finished cooking, heat the olive oil in a wide saucepan over a low heat. Gently sauté the garlic for about 1 minute, just until it's fragrant but not browned. Stir in the chilli flakes.

Remove a cup of water from the boiling pasta pot, then drain the pasta well and add it to the garlic and chilli in the pan. Mix well and add a little of the reserved pasta cooking water if it looks too dry. Season with salt and serve immediately.

SERVES 4–6

500g spaghetti
12 tablespoons extra virgin olive oil
4 garlic cloves, peeled and left whole
1 level teaspoon dried chilli flakes
salt

Velvety vegetable soup with Altamura crostini

Una vellutata di verdure

When you want to offer your guests something small, warm and nutritious, a *vellutata* is appreciated. This is a blended minestrone soup.

HEAT THE OIL in a saucepan over a medium heat. Sweat the onions in the oil for about 5 minutes, until they start to soften. Add the rest of the vegetables except the courgettes and potato. Pour in the water and a generous seasoning of salt and pepper and bring up to a simmer. Cover and cook over a medium heat for 10 minutes, then add the courgettes and potato and cook for another 10 minutes. Remove from the heat and allow to cool a little before stirring in the grated parmigiano. Using a hand blender, blitz the soup to a velvety consistency.

Toast the bread on both sides. Ladle the soup into small soup bowls with a swirl of cream or a knob of goat's cheese on top, if using. Serve with a slice of toast on the side and garnish with a little fresh parsley.

SERVES 12

4 tablespoons extra virgin olive oil

2 medium onions, diced

2 medium carrots, diced

2 celery sticks, diced

2 ripe beef tomatoes, chopped

150g French beans, cut in half

2 litres cold water

salt and freshly ground black pepper

2 courgettes, diced

1 medium potato, diced

20g freshly grated parmigiano (optional)

12 small slices of Altamura bread or sourdough bread, cut 1cm thick

120ml fresh cream or 50g goat's cheese (optional)

1 tablespoon finely chopped fresh flat-leaf parsley

You might decide not to blend the soup, in which case I recommend adding a tin of strained chickpeas, lentils or borlotti beans to the pot 5 minutes before serving.

Zio Mario's eggs and peas

Uova in cappotto di piselli

Zio Mario and Aunt Jean are two geniuses in the kitchen. They can make even a simple slice of buttered toast into something marvellous. The bread will have been carefully chosen and toasted just right – crunchy on the outside and soft on the inside; the butter will have been sourced with the same enthusiasm as choosing truffles; and the butter is spread in such a way that it doesn't melt immediately and little blobs remain bubbling on the surface. The result is an unforgettable morsel.

Mario's days are filled with sourcing foodstuffs, and while his culinary talents are extraordinary, it's his simple dishes that I love best. I have many memories of my sister Pat and myself, with a group of friends in tow, arriving at their house unexpectedly and very late from a distant *festa*. Jean and Mario would rustle up something tasty, Jean discharging the orders and Mario executing them with enthusiasm. Invariably a bottle (or two) of white wine would appear that he had picked up that day from some unknown winery.

HEAT THE OIL in a wide saucepan over a low heat. Sweat the shallot in the oil for about 5 minutes, until it just starts to soften, then add the passata or tinned tomatoes and season with salt. Simmer for 5 minutes more.

Meanwhile, immerse the peas in boiling salted water and cook for 5 minutes. Drain and add the peas to the sauce.

Make four small wells in the sauce in the pan and break an egg into each one. Cover for a couple of minutes, until the whites are perfectly set and the yolks are still runny.

Serve with Pecorino or parmigiano shavings, a pinch of salt and a grinding of black pepper and crusty bread, of course.

SERVES 2–4

4 tablespoons extra virgin olive oil
1 shallot, finely sliced
250ml tomato passata or 1 x 400g tin of whole plum tomatoes (mash the tomatoes in a bowl with a fork)
salt and freshly ground black pepper
250g frozen peas or leftover cooked peas
4 free-range or organic eggs
50g Pecorino or parmigiano shavings
crusty bread, to serve

This recipe sets out how to make the dish from scratch, but it's really meant to be made with whatever leftover sauce you might have in the fridge, such as pomodoro, amatriciana *or even* arrabbiata *sauce.*

Ciambellini wine biscotti

Ciambellini biscuits were traditionally eaten at Easter because their circular shape recalls the Christian crown of thorns, but nowadays they are consumed all year round. They are particularly delicious dunked in wine after a heavy lunch or dinner instead of a creamy dessert. The best I have eaten are at Da Armando al Pantheon in Salita de' Crescenzi beside the Pantheon in Rome. Da Armando al Pantheon offers the best of traditional Roman fare and is one of my *ritroui* – a place where I meet up with Italian friends.

MAKES ABOUT 40 BISCUITS

500g self-raising flour
150g caster sugar, plus extra for
    coating
1 level teaspoon baking powder
zest of 1 lemon
pinch of salt
150ml dry white wine
100ml extra virgin olive oil

PREHEAT THE OVEN to 180℃. Line two baking trays with parchment paper.

Lightly mix the flour, sugar, baking powder, lemon zest and a pinch of salt in a large bowl, then stir in the wine and oil. Knead well on a lightly floured work surface for about 5 minutes, forming the pastry into a ball.

Break off small knobs of pastry and roll each piece into a small snake that is 18cm long and 2cm thick. Form into a circle and repeat with the rest of the pastry. You should make about 40 biscuits.

Pour some caster sugar into a shallow bowl. Dip each circle into the sugar, coating one side only. Place the biscuits, sugar side up, on the lined trays, leaving a 2cm gap between each biscuit. Bake for 25 minutes, until golden. Cool on a wire rack.

Serve with a dessert wine such as vin santo, a Zibibbo or a good red wine. Suggest to your guests that they try dunking the biscuits in the wine. These will keep for up to a week in an airtight container.

CARNEVALE LATE AFTERNOON BUFFET LUNCH IN MASQUERADE

Un Buffet per Carnevale in Maschera

PRESENT

Family, friends and lots of pirates, princesses and pilots

ANTIPASTO

Canapés with smoked salmon, soft goat's cheese, rocket and candied orange

PASTA

Timballo of pasta with tomato, speck and aubergine

Children's tomato sauce with hidden vegetables

TORTA RUSTICA

Spinach, ricotta and pine nut tart

MAINS

Courgette and speck frittata

Porcini meatloaf with truffle oil and tomato sauce

Pizza margherita with finnochiona salami

SIDES

Allegria salad

DESSERT

Castagnole mini doughnuts

Frappe

Nutella pizza

IN RESPONSE to my laments on

the insurmountable bureaucracy involved in restoring a tiny apartment in Venice, an email from an Irish friend beautifully describes the Venetian tempo:

Eileen, you must understand that La Bella Venezia is lost in time. The mists from the sea create a dream world where there is no rush, no anxiety, no stress at all. Everything floats along in the shimmering waters of the lagoon in perfect contentment. The concept of time is for others – less fortunate people like ourselves.

You will understand this when you start to live there and evolve into a true Venetian. So do not worry about the work to be done. The Cosmos will decide when the time is right for it to happen. Until then, just look forward to the tranquillity that awaits you in La Serenissima!

Venice is the epicentre of Italian *carnevale*, a time when the city transforms into a unique stage of props, proms and palaver, where inhibitions are abandoned and locals and tourists unite as thespians at masquerade performances. Venetian masks are reverently crafted and portray traditional historical characters. They are requisite, elaborate and mesmerising.

Although *carnevale* starts the day after the Epiphany on 6 January (or 12 days after Christmas), the exciting celebrations take place the week before *Martedì Grasso*, or Shrove Tuesday. Towns and villages all over Italy enact *carnevale* processions called *sfilate*. Viareggio hosts the most elaborate and magical of all the *carnevale* parades. Adorned *carri* (floats) parade through the town followed by locals dressed in masquerade. Hordes of small children throw colourful paper *coriandoli* (confetti), while further down the coast in Rome, mischievous teenagers throw eggs at unsuspecting adults – tourists beware!

Children go to numerous parties during *carnevale*, and a buffet party of finger food is ideal for young pirates, princesses and pilots.

Canapés with smoked salmon, soft goat's cheese, rocket and candied orange

Canapé con salmone affumicato, caprino, rucola e scorza d'arancia candita

Sweet candied orange is a lovely contrast with the saltiness of the smoked salmon. This is my baroque canapé – ostentatious, provocative and truly carnivalesque.

FIRST MAKE THE CANDIED ORANGE. Remove the peel from the oranges in big pieces and cut into 1cm x 6cm strips. Blanch the peel in boiling water for a couple of minutes and drain. Simmer the sugar and water in a small saucepan until the sugar dissolves, then add the peel. Cover and simmer over a low heat for 45 minutes. Remove the peel with a slotted spoon and leave to cool on a wire rack overnight.

The next day, toast the bread on both sides, remove the crust and cut each slice into four pieces. When cool, spread each slice with goat's cheese and top with a little rocket and a slice of smoked salmon. Top with two pieces of candied orange.

MAKES 24

6 thick slices of sliced pan
100g soft goat's cheese
bunch of fresh rocket
500g thinly sliced Irish smoked
    salmon

For the candied orange:
2 oranges
30g caster sugar
250ml water

Make extra candied orange and dip it in melted chocolate for a lovely treat served with herbal tea at the end of a meal.

Timballo of pasta with tomato, speck and aubergine

Timballo di pasta con pomodoro, speck and melanzane

Italians rarely throw out food. What is left over from a meal is not treated as mere leftovers, but rather as a precious ingredient to be transformed into something equally as good as the original. A *timballo* of pasta is usually a combination of whatever ingredients you find when you open your fridge, majestically put together to create a wonderful new dish.

Italian etiquette requires that you compliment your host effusively on his or her cooking skills, request the recipes and take home a helping of your favourite dish. So when your host tells you with a touch of due elegance, '*Ho fatto un timballo di pasta buonissimo*' (I made a very tasty *timballo* of pasta), you should reply, '*Fantastico, sará davvero buonissimo.*' (Fantastic, it will truly be very tasty.) Compare that to 'I rustled up a pasta bake with some leftovers' – a real appetite extinguisher!

HEAT THE OLIVE OIL in a large saucepan over a low heat. Sauté the garlic for about 1 minute, just until it's fragrant but not browned. Add the diced aubergines, cover and cook for about 20 minutes, until the aubergines soften and are nicely browned. Remove the aubergines with a slotted spoon and drain on some kitchen paper.

Meanwhile, make the sauce. Heat the olive oil in a wide, heavy-based saucepan over a low heat. Sweat the shallots for about 5 minutes, until they are soft and translucent.

Continued overleaf

SERVES 6–8

6 tablespoons extra virgin olive oil

2 garlic cloves, thinly sliced

2 aubergines, diced into 2cm cubes

500g dried pasta

250g mozzarella, diced

200g speck, pancetta or leftover cooked ham, sliced thinly and diced

50g freshly grated parmigiano

For the tomato sauce:

4 tablespoons extra virgin olive oil

2 shallots, finely sliced

2 x 400g tins of whole plum tomatoes

2 fresh ripe plum tomatoes, chopped

4 fresh basil leaves

1 teaspoon salt

Place the tinned tomatoes in a bowl and mash them with a fork. Add the tomatoes to the saucepan along with the fresh tomatoes, basil and salt. Stir, cover and cook for 15 minutes. Blend with a hand blender.

When the aubergines are getting towards the end of their cooking time, preheat the oven to 200℃.

Cook the pasta in a large saucepan of boiling salted water until al dente or according to the packet instructions. Drain and place in a 30cm x 20cm casserole dish that is 12cm deep. Pour over 250ml of the tomato sauce and mix well (use the rest of the sauce with some pasta another time).

Add the aubergines, mozzarella, speck and parmigiano to the pasta in the casserole dish and mix well. Place in the hot oven and bake for 15 minutes. Remove from the dish and leave to cool and settle. Cut into thick wedges and serve on a platter.

You can use leftover pasta from the previous day and incorporate a variety of vegetables, such as courgettes, peppers, mushrooms or broccoli. If you can't find speck, pancetta, prosciutto or leftover cooked ham would work well too. Cheese and fresh herbs are a nice touch.

Children's tomato sauce with hidden vegetables

Sugo di pomodoro con verdure nascoste

Italians are quite obsessive when it comes to children's diets, and kids' parties require good, wholesome food or you risk the ire of visiting mums and dads, who rarely simply drop off little Tomasso or Alessandra. Parents tend to stay too, so make enough food for everyone. When our children were small, Stefano, equally obsessed, would make this sauce to ensure they ate enough vegetables.

COOK THE CAULIFLOWER in boiling salted water for 5 minutes. Drain.

Heat the olive oil in a wide, heavy-based saucepan over a low heat. Sweat the shallots for about 5 minutes, until they are soft and translucent.

Place the tinned tomatoes in a bowl and mash them with a fork. Add the tomatoes to the saucepan along with the fresh tomatoes, carrot batons, basil and salt. Cover and cook for 10 minutes. Add the cauliflower and cook for an additional 5 minutes. Blend with a hand blender.

Serve on pasta if you have a fussy little eater. Children enjoy farfalle and pastina is ideal for infants.

MAKES ENOUGH SAUCE FOR
10 PORTIONS OF PASTA

1 head of cauliflower or broccoli,
    broken into florets
4 tablespoons extra virgin olive oil
2 shallots, finely sliced
2 x 400g tins of whole plum
    tomatoes
2 fresh ripe plum tomatoes,
    chopped
2 carrots, cut into batons
4 fresh basil leaves
1 teaspoon salt

Spinach, ricotta and pine nut tart

Torta rustica di spinaci, ricotta e pinoli

Invariably, *torta rustica* (sometimes called *torta salata*, or salty cake) is a quick and easy solution, especially if frozen pastry is used, for busy households where both parents hold down demanding jobs requiring long hours away from home. *Torta rustica* is one of those dishes that I don't tend to make very often myself, so I really enjoy it when dining at friends' homes. When my Milanese friends send an invite, I just know it's going to be a delicious *torta rustica*.

USING YOUR FINGERS, mix the butter through the flour until it resembles fine breadcrumbs. Add one beaten egg and mix to form a soft dough. Wrap in cling film and leave to rest in the fridge for 1 hour.

Preheat the oven to 180℃. Grease a deep 23cm circular dish with a little butter (use a fluted dish for a fancy finish).

Remove the pastry from the cling film and cut in half. On a lightly floured board, roll out the first ball so that you have enough to line the base and sides of the dish. You can bake it blind, but Italians don't tend to do this since the tart is eaten as soon as it comes out of the oven.

SERVES 6

For the pastry
   (*or use frozen pastry*):
100g butter, cut into cubes, plus
   extra for greasing
175g plain flour
2 free-range or organic eggs

For the filling:
50g pine nuts
500g spinach leaves, washed
250g fresh ricotta
100g freshly grated parmigiano
1 free-range or organic egg, beaten
zest of 1 orange
salt and freshly ground black pepper

Toast the pine nuts on a hot, dry pan for 30 seconds, taking care not to let them burn. Tip into a bowl and set aside.

Immerse the spinach in boiling salted water for a couple of minutes. Drain very well.

Combine the spinach, ricotta, parmigiano, beaten egg, orange zest and the toasted pine nuts with some salt and pepper in a mixing bowl. Pour the mixture into the pastry-lined dish.

Roll out the remaining pastry and cut into strips 2cm wide. Lay them across the top of the tart in a criss-cross pattern, creating a lattice effect. Lightly beat the remaining egg and glaze the pastry with it.

Bake in the hot oven for 30 minutes, until the pastry is light golden. Allow to stand for 5–10 minutes before cutting into wedges to serve.

You can use a variety of fillings, such as Swiss chard and ricotta, cooked ham and smoked mozzarella, or Swiss chard, radicchio and scarmorza. You can also use frozen puff pastry or a savoury pastry. It's worth noting that when cooking Swiss chard, you should cut the stalks from the leaves and cook them separately because the leaves cook in a couple of minutes, while the stalks can take up to 10 minutes.

Courgette and speck frittata

Frittata con zucchine, porri e speck

Italian parents spend a lot of money on *carnevale* costumes, but they are well used. They get passed on from sibling to sibling, or as happened in our family, from Stefano to our son Ghinlon and then to his son Tristan, and I presume Odhran will have the well-worn and much-loved d'Artagnan outfit next.

Stefano's frittata is a family favourite of ours. It's delicious served piping hot with toasted ciabatta and a simple salad, or you can serve it at room temperature for buffet lunches or pre-dinner drinks.

HEAT 2 TABLESPOONS of the olive oil in a large pan over a low heat. Sauté the shallots for about 5 minutes, until they are soft and translucent. Add the speck and courgettes and cook for about 10 minutes, stirring regularly. Leave to cool slightly.

Beat the eggs in a large bowl, then stir in the shallots, speck and courgettes along with the parmigiano. Season with salt and pepper and mix well to combine.

Heat the remaining 2 tablespoons of oil in a large (28cm) non-stick pan over a medium heat and pour in the egg mixture, tipping the pan to spread the eggs evenly. Cook for 3 minutes, until the eggs are set.

Gently pull the frittata from the edges of the pan. Place a large dinner plate over the pan and turn it over so that the frittata is now sitting on the plate. Slide the frittata back into the pan to cook the other side for about 2 minutes.

Slide the frittata onto a serving plate or cut into wedges.

SERVES 6

4 tablespoons extra virgin olive oil
2 shallots, finely sliced
50g speck, pancetta, prosciutto, guanciale or cooked ham, sliced finely and chopped
4 medium courgettes, thinly sliced
8 free-range or organic eggs, beaten
50g freshly grated parmigiano
salt and freshly ground black pepper

Other variations worth trying are mushrooms and pancetta or leeks, cherry tomatoes and scarmorza or smoked mozzarella.

Porcini meatloaf with truffle oil and tomato sauce

Polpettone con porcini e olio tartufato

SOAK THE DRIED PORCINI in the milk and a little hot water for at least 2 hours. Remove the mushrooms from the milk and chop them roughly. Strain the milk and set aside to use later in the sauce.

In a mixing bowl, combine the minced beef with half of the porcini along with the breadcrumbs, parmigiano, sliced shallots, beaten egg, truffle oil and some salt and pepper. Use your hands to get a nice smooth finish.

Place the mixture onto a lightly floured board and flatten it into a rectangle. Place the slices of prosciutto lengthways down the middle and scatter the rest of the porcini on top. Close over and roll to create a thick snake shape while securing the stuffing inside. Wrap in cling film and refrigerate for 1 hour.

Heat the olive oil in a wide saucepan (one that the meatloaf will fit into later on) over a low heat. Sauté the shallots, carrots, celery, bay leaves and rosemary for 5 minutes, until softened. Add the speck and leave it to colour for 1 minute, then pour in the wine and increase the heat momentarily to cook off the alcohol. Stir in the tomatoes and the strained milk and season with salt.

Remove the meatloaf from the cling film and place it gently in the pan. Spoon over the sauce, cover and cook for about 90 minutes on a low heat. Continue to spoon over the sauce regularly and add some warm water if it looks like it's getting too dry.

Leave to rest for 10 minutes. Slice into thick circles, spoon over the sauce and serve.

SERVES 6–8

50g dried porcini mushrooms
250ml milk
500g minced beef
100g fresh breadcrumbs
20g freshly grated parmigiano
2 shallots, finely sliced
1 free-range or organic egg, beaten
1 level tablespoon black truffle oil
salt and freshly ground black
   pepper
2 slices of prosciutto

For the tomato sauce:
4 tablespoons extra virgin olive oil
2 shallots, finely sliced
1 carrot, finely diced
1 celery stick, finely diced
2 bay leaves
sprig of fresh rosemary
50g thinly sliced speck, shredded
150ml red wine
1 x 400g tin of cherry tomatoes
salt

A little creative flair can change an everyday, somewhat boring dish into something special.

Pizza margherita with finocchiona salami

Pizzette con salame finnochiona

The Forno at Campo di Fiore in Rome still makes the best *pizza bianca* (white pizza) in the world. It's a kind of salty flatbread dotted with rock salt and drizzled with olive oil, to be eaten hot from the oven, or later, when cooled, sliced open and filled with prosciutto, bresaola, Asiago cheese, mashed fresh figs or whatever takes your fancy.

Grab a good chunk of *pizza bianca*, fill a bottle of cool refreshing water from the ancient water fountain sitting conveniently beside the dazzling flower stalls and pop over to Piazza Farnese. Take your seat at the base of one of the huge fountains hauled from the Baths of Caracalla and gaze through the windows of the Palazzo Farnese. Many's the hour I have passed there, enthralled by the frescos glimpsed through those enormous, prohibitive panes and dreaming of walking under Caracci's *Loves of the Gods.*

I thought it opportune to discuss my pizza recipe with my good Neapolitan friend, Giuseppina Energe. Giuseppina has three sons and one grandson and all but one son live abroad. She does, however, have lots of siblings, relatives and friends living close to her in Vomero, so she would not recommend making anything less than two large oven trays of pizza. This is her recipe. Even though Italian families are relatively small – they have one of the lowest birth rates in Europe – cooking nevertheless continues to be for large groups. Meals are meant to be shared with extended family and neighbours who just might be alone. All are welcome.

Continued overleaf

MAKES 2 LARGE PIZZAS

For the pizza dough:
1 x 7g sachet fast action dried yeast
1 teaspoon caster sugar
250ml warm water
500g strong white flour
2 tablespoons extra virgin olive oil
pinch of salt
butter, for greasing the oven trays

For the sauce:
500ml tomato passata or tomato
    sauce
2 tablespoons extra virgin olive oil
1 level teaspoon salt

For the topping:
300g buffalo mozzarella, diced
100g thinly sliced finocchiona
    salami
bunch of fresh basil leaves

To make the pizza dough, dissolve the yeast and sugar in the warm water in a small bowl and let it stand for 10 minutes, until the yeast is frothy.

Pour the flour onto a wooden board and form a mound. Make a well in the middle of the mound and pour the activated yeast mixture, oil and salt into the well. Using your fingers, start to mix the flour with the liquid. Start around the edges of the well and gradually incorporate all of the flour. Knead the dough for a good 10 minutes, until it's smooth and elastic. Alternatively, you could use a food mixer fitted with a dough hook.

Brush two large bowls for proving the dough with a little olive oil. Divide the dough in half and knead again to form two smooth balls. Place each ball in an oiled bowl and cover with a clean, damp cloth. Leave to rise in a warm place for about 2 hours, until the dough has doubled in size.

Meanwhile, to make the sauce, simply stir the oil and salt into the tomato passata. Drain the mozzarella in a colander to remove the excess moisture.

Preheat the oven to 220°C. Grease two large baking trays with butter.

Turn the dough out onto a floured surface. Knock it back and knead for a couple of minutes.

Roll out each piece until it's 0.5cm thick – you want a wafer-thin base (contrary to Giuseppina, who prefers a thick base). Using your hands, stretch the dough to cover each tray. Make little indents all over the top using your fingertips.

Spread the sauce over the two trays of pizza. Bake in the oven for 20 minutes. Using a knife, lift the pizza up and peek underneath – it should be golden. Remove from the oven and dot with the drained mozzarella, salami and basil. Return to the oven for another 5 minutes, until the mozzarella has melted. Cut into small or large squares with a big pair of scissors. Serve hot.

The combinations of pizza toppings are endless. You might like to add some vegetables (make sure greens, such as spinach, have been well drained of any moisture), various types of cheese or salumi, walnuts or pine nuts. One of my own favourite combinations is potato (use diced, cooked potatoes), Tuscan sausage and goat's cheese (drained of excess moisture).

You can reheat pizza by placing it on a very hot unoiled pan or in a hot oven for a couple of minutes.

Allegria salad

Insalata allegra

'*Portano allegria*,' Nonna would say as she watched the children playing in the courtyard beneath her shuttered window – they bring joy. *Allegria* – just the sound of the word makes one happy and joyful.

PLACE THE EGGS in a saucepan and cover well with cold water. Bring to the boil, then cover the pan and remove it from the heat. Leave to stand for 12 minutes. Remove the eggs from the water with a slotted spoon and run under cold water to cool them quickly. Once cooled, peel the eggs.

Bring a pot of salted water to a boil. Tip in the French beans and boil for 3–4 minutes, until al dente. Drain and refresh under cold running water so that they keep their vibrant green colour.

Prepare the dressing by placing all of the ingredients in a screw-top jar and shaking well to mix.

Place the salad leaves, goat's cheese, French beans and walnuts in a large serving bowl. Pour the dressing over the salad and toss.

Cut the hard-boiled eggs in half and place on top of the salad. Serve immediately.

SERVES 8

8 free-range or organic eggs
200g French beans
500g seasonal salad leaves (such as radicchio, rocket or Little Gem), washed and dried
400g soft goat's cheese, crumbled
50g shelled walnuts

For the dressing:
200ml extra virgin olive oil
2 tablespoons honey
juice of 1 lemon
pinch of salt

Do not dress salads until it's time to serve them, otherwise the leaves will wilt.

Castagnole mini doughnuts

Castagnole

I have to warn you, these are addictive, calorific and wonderful. It's just as well they only make an appearance once a year!

CREAM THE SUGAR, butter and lemon zest together until it's light and fluffy, then add the beaten eggs, mixing well to incorporate them.

Whisk together the flour and salt in a separate bowl, then add to the wet ingredients and mix until just combined.

Turn the dough out onto a lightly floured board and roll into a thick snake. Cut the snake into 3cm pieces. Roll each piece between the palms of your hands to form small balls.

Heat the oil in a large saucepan or a deep-fat fryer until it reaches 175℃. Test the heat by dropping a small piece of dough into the hot oil – it should quickly turn golden.

Fry the balls in batches of four in the hot oil. Remove with a slotted spoon and drain on a plate lined with kitchen paper to remove the excess oil. Place on a serving plate and dust with icing sugar.

These are lovely served warm, but they're also nice when cooled. These mini doughnuts can be kept in an airtight container for up to three days.

MAKES 40

80g granulated sugar
60g butter, softened
zest of 1 lemon
3 free-range or organic eggs, beaten
370g self-raising flour
pinch of salt
1 litre nut oil or sunflower oil, for frying
icing sugar, for dusting

Frappe

Marvellously crispy, light and sweet, there is never enough! These are known as *frappe* in Rome, *chiacchiere* (small talk) south of Rome and *bugie* (lies) in northern Italy.

My firstborn came into the world during *carnevale* against a surreal backdrop of a vivid full moon that softened his deliciously rosy cheeks. Visitors brought me trays of *frappe* and *castagnole* from the very best pastry shop on Viale Europa and I never wanted to leave the pampering nurses, who would ask, 'What would you like for lunch today: linguine with artichokes or prosciutto tortellini in broth?'

PLACE A MOUND OF FLOUR on a pastry board and form a well in the middle. Put the butter, beaten eggs, lemon zest and a pinch of salt in the well and mix using your fingers. Start by taking flour from the sides and gradually incorporate all of the flour. Work the dough for 5 minutes and form a neat ball.

Lightly grease a mixing bowl with butter. Place the dough in the bowl, cover with cling film and place in the fridge for 1 hour or so.

MAKES 40

200g plain flour
40g butter, diced and softened
2 free-range or organic eggs,
    beaten
zest of 1 lemon
pinch of salt
1 litre nut oil, for frying
runny honey, for drizzling
icing sugar, for dusting

Roll out the dough on a lightly floured board as thinly as possible with a rolling pin. If you have a pasta machine, pass it through the thinnest setting a couple of times.

Cut the dough into strips 4cm wide, then cut the strips into pieces 4cm long.

Heat the oil in a large saucepan or deep-fat fryer until it reaches 165–170°C. Test the heat by dropping a small piece of dough into the hot oil – it should quickly turn golden.

Fry the *frappe* in the sizzling oil until the strips take on a nice golden colour – this only takes a few seconds. Remove with a slotted spoon and place on a plate lined with kitchen paper to remove the excess oil.

Place on a serving platter, drizzle with honey and sprinkle with icing sugar. Serve warm or cold. These will keep in an airtight container for up to three days.

Nutella pizza

Pizza con Nutella

I was chatting with my editor about our favourite little village in the Marche and how the local *pizzaiolo*, delighted to see the children back each summer, would treat them to pizza with Nutella. 'We must have that in the book!' she said, so here is the recipe, a winner with children everywhere. But now that I have grabbed your attention, I must recommend that you use a really good chocolate with a high cocoa solid content instead of Nutella.

TO MAKE THE PIZZA DOUGH, dissolve the yeast and sugar in the warm water in a small bowl and let it stand for 10 minutes, until the yeast is frothy.

Pour the flour onto a wooden board and form a mound. Make a well in the middle of the mound and pour the activated yeast mixture, oil and salt into the well. Using your fingers, start to mix the flour with the liquid. Start around the edges of the well and gradually incorporate all of the flour. Knead the dough for a good 10 minutes, until it's smooth and elastic. Alternatively, you could use a food mixer fitted with a dough hook.

Brush a large bowl for proving the dough with olive oil. Form the dough into a smooth ball, place in the oiled bowl and cover with a clean, damp cloth. Leave to rise in a warm place for about 2 hours, until the dough has doubled in size.

MAKES 2 LARGE PIZZAS

1 x 7g sachet fast action dried yeast
1 teaspoon caster sugar
250ml warm water
500g plain flour
2 tablespoons extra virgin olive oil
pinch of salt
knob of butter, for greasing
200g Nutella or 250g good-quality
    dark chocolate (at least 70% cocoa
    solids)
icing sugar, for dusting

Preheat the oven to 200℃. Grease two large baking trays with butter.

Turn the dough out onto a floured surface. Knock it back and knead for a couple of minutes. Roll out the dough until it's 0.5cm thick. Using your hands, stretch the dough to fit the two greased trays. Bake in the hot oven for 20–25 minutes.

If using dark chocolate instead of Nutella, melt the chocolate in a heatproof bowl set over a pan of gently simmering water (a bain-marie), making sure the water doesn't touch the bottom of the bowl. Stir until smooth.

Remove the base from the oven and spread with the melted chocolate or Nutella. Use a sieve to sprinkle with icing sugar. Leave to rest for a couple of minutes before cutting into squares or rectangles. This is nicest when served warm.

A ROMANTIC DINNER FOR ST VALENTINE'S DAY

Una Cena Romantica per San Valentino

PRESENT

Two couples

....

ANTIPASTO

Walnut, prune and pancetta caramels

PASTA

Spaghetti with clams and courgette pesto

Risotto with courgette flowers, peas and walnuts

MAINS

Monkfish with rosemary chickpeas and crispy prosciutto

Veal *straccetti* with sage and culatello di zibello

SIDES

Heirloom tomato, rocket and carpaccio of mushroom salad

DESSERT

Pannacotta with passion fruit coulis

MY HUSBAND, Stefano, jokes

that I was the easiest person to woo – a good dinner did the trick! I don't agree, of course. Italians are notoriously and irresistibly romantic.

Our first dinner together was at his apartment, a converted former *lavatoio*, or communal laundry room, with an enormous terrace overlooking a tapestry of terracotta rooftops – a wondrous view of old Rome in all its glory. Who could resist such a view? Communal laundry rooms were common in old buildings. Situated on the top floor, they housed a wash area consisting of a concrete or marble sink that incorporated a scrubbing board with an indent for the carbolic soap. Outside there is a huge terrace where residents hung out their washing to dry, with a wash line allotted to each family. In the past these terraces offered housewives a haven of friendship, a place to discuss *i mariti* (husbands) and *la famiglia* (the family) and to exchange recipes. One of my favourite films, *Una Giornata Particolare*, starring Sophia Loren and Marcello Mastroianni, features a poignant scene on a similar roof terrace among lines of well-scrubbed washing. If you are looking for a pied-à-terre in the sky with a huge terrace, search for an abandoned *lavatoio*. They are largely unused nowadays and condominiums can be convinced to sell.

Stefano cooked a superb dinner that night, and the climb to the fifth floor was worth every morsel. It was a special night, as it was also the first time I met Stefano's best friend, Daniele Archibugi, a colourful, stimulating and quintessential professor, including bushy eyebrows, who never fails to provoke, and his future wife, Paola, a young university professor and expert in Russian literature. Paola was and continues to be stunningly beautiful and I don't doubt Modigliani would have yearned to paint her. Friendships are important – they keep us anchored. Regardless of how many miles are between us or how many years pass by, Daniele and Stefano stay in touch regularly and it's nice to know Stefano has someone to confide in.

Walnut, prune and pancetta caramels

Caramelle di prugne, nocciole e pancetta

My favourite place to visit in Umbria is the Antonelli winery, a stone's throw from the gorgeous historic town of Montefalco. Filippo Antonelli runs a cookery school on the grounds of his vineyard and the place is always a hive of activity. I am usually greeted with a large glass of his world-renowned Sagrantino red wine and prune *caramelle* and a long story on the lastest *vendemmia* (harvest). No matter how busy Filippo is, he manages to make everyone feel so welcome.

STUFF EACH PRUNE with a walnut and wrap in pancetta.

Heat the olive oil in a large pan over a medium heat. Fry batches of the stuffed prunes for 2 minutes on each side, until the pancetta crisps up. Serve warm or cold.

MAKES 24

24 dried pitted prunes
24 blanched walnuts
50g thinly sliced pancetta, shredded
4 tablespoons extra virgin olive oil

Spaghetti with clams and courgette pesto

Spaghetti con vongole e pesto di zucchine

Italians aren't afraid to use their hands when eating. Each shelled clam is picked from the plate, the fish sucked out and the empty shell flung into a recipient bowl with a delightful cling. Food, gestures and gossip, clinks and chatter are a recipe for warm, congenial dinners.

CHECK THAT THE CLAMS ARE ALL CLOSED. If you find an opened one, tap it on the side of a plate – it should close, but if it remains open, discard it. Steep the clams in a large bowl of cold water with a pinch of salt and change the water several times until you're ready to use them.

To make the courgette pesto, cut a thin slice off the ends of the courgettes and discard. Slice the courgettes and place in a blender along with half of the garlic, all of the Pecorino and 4 tablespoons of the olive oil. Blitz until it's a nice runny consistency.

Cook the spaghetti in a large saucepan of boiling salted water until al dente or according to the packet instructions.

Heat the remaining 4 tablespoons of olive oil in a wide pan or wok over a low heat. Sauté the remaining garlic for about 1 minute, just until the garlic is fragrant but not browned. Add the clams and pour in the wine. Increase the heat momentarily to cook off the alcohol, then cover the pan for a couple of minutes. The clams are ready when they have all opened. Discard any unopened clams. Remove the clams from their shells and strain the pan juices through a sieve. (You can enjoy a couple clams while you do this!)

In a separate large saucepan, gently heat the courgette pesto. Combine the clams, their cooking juices and the courgette pesto. Drain the pasta and put it in a large serving bowl. Add in the pesto and the clams and mix well. Serve immediately.

SERVES 4–6

1kg fresh clams
500g courgettes
4 garlic cloves, chopped
50g freshly grated Pecorino
8 tablespoons extra virgin
    olive oil
500g spaghetti
100ml white wine

Brainse Ráth Maonais
Rathmines Branch
Fón / Tel: 4973539

Risotto with courgette flowers, peas and walnuts

Risotto con fiori di zucchine, piselli e noci

Courgette flowers are a beauty to behold. You barely breathe and they have disappeared. They are to be handled with the utmost care and respect.

To make the broth, fill a saucepan with 1 litre of cold water and add in the vegetables and the salt and pepper. Cover the pan and bring to a boil, then reduce the heat and simmer for 30 minutes. Remove the vegetables with a slotted spoon and discard them (or you could eat them dressed with a little olive oil). Keep the broth hot.

To make the risotto, cook the peas in boiling salted water for a couple of minutes, drain and set aside. Chop the courgette flowers delicately into strips.

Heat the olive oil in a large, wide, heavy-based saucepan over a low heat. Sweat the shallots in the oil for about 5 minutes, until they are soft and translucent. Add the rice to the saucepan and allow it to toast in the oil for a couple of minutes, until it starts to turn translucent. Pour in the wine and increase the heat momentarily to cook off the alcohol. Stir in 50g of the peas.

Add the hot broth one ladleful at a time. Stir constantly until all the broth has been absorbed before adding the next ladle. Keep adding the broth bit by bit and stirring until all the broth has been absorbed, which should take about 20 minutes.

When the rice is cooked but still has a bite, fold in the cream along with the rest of the peas, the shredded flowers, crushed walnuts, parmigiano and butter. Serve immediately and garnish each serving with a deep-fried courgette flower.

Serves 6

300g frozen or fresh peas
6 courgettes with flowers, plus extra
    flowers to garnish
4 tablespoons extra virgin olive oil
2 shallots, finely chopped
360g Carnaroli or Vialone Nano rice
200ml dry white wine
150ml cream
50g crushed walnuts
50g freshly grated parmigiano
50g butter

For the broth:
1 litre cold water
1 onion, peeled and left whole
1 carrot, peeled and left whole
1 beef tomato
1 celery stick
1 heaped tablespoon salt
freshly ground black pepper

Risotto should not have a mushy consistency – the rice should still have a nice bite. The creaminess comes from the starch that is released from the rice combined with the parmigiano and butter that are stirred through at the end.

Monkfish with rosemary chickpeas and crispy prosciutto

Coda di rospo con ceci al rosmarino e prosciutto croccante

This is a favourite dish of mine and every forkful takes me back to our times in the Marche. Marchigiani people are geniuses when it comes to combining seafood with pulses, a combination known as *mari e monti* (seas and mountains).

IF YOU ARE USING DRIED CHICKPEAS, place them in a large saucepan of cold water overnight. The next day, drain and rinse under cold running water. Fill a large saucepan with 2 litres of cold water and add in the chickpeas, onion, carrot, celery, a sprig of rosemary and the salt. Bring to the boil, then lower the heat and simmer for 45 minutes to 1 hour, until the chickpeas are soft but not mushy. Remove the vegetables and the rosemary sprig and discard. Drain the chickpeas, but keep back a mug of the cooking broth (you can retain the stock as a soup base). Or if you are using tinned chickpeas, simply drain and rinse before use.

Place the drained chickpeas and a couple of spoons of broth in a blender and blitz to a velvety consistency. If you are using tinned chickpeas, just include a couple of spoons of warm water. Season to taste.

SERVES 6

4 tablespoons extra virgin olive oil
4 garlic cloves, 2 cloves thinly sliced and 2 cloves peeled and left whole
1 teaspoon dried chilli flakes
400ml dry white wine
6 x 200g monkfish chunks
200g prosciutto, cut into strips
salt and freshly ground black pepper
6 small sprigs of fresh rosemary, to garnish

For the chickpea vellutata:
250g dried chickpeas or 2 x 400g tins of chickpeas
1 onion, peeled and left whole
1 carrot, peeled and left whole
1 celery stick
sprig of fresh rosemary
1 level teaspoon salt

Heat 2 tablespoons of the olive oil in a wide, heavy-based saucepan over a low heat. Sauté the sliced garlic for about 1 minute, just until it's fragrant but not browned. Stir in the chilli flakes and chickpea *vellutata*. Pour in 200ml of the wine and increase the heat momentarily to cook off the alcohol.

In a separate large pan, heat the remaining 2 tablespoons of olive oil over a low heat. Sauté the 2 whole garlic cloves for about 1 minute, just until it's fragrant and has flavoured the oil. Remove the garlic with a slotted spoon.

Seal the monkfish by cooking it in the garlic-infused oil for 1 minute on each side. Pour in the rest of the wine and increase the heat momentarily to cook off the alcohol. Cover and cook for 5 minutes.

Meanwhile, cook the prosciutto strips on a hot, dry pan until they are crispy.

To serve, coat the base of six pasta bowls with the chickpea *vellutata*. Place a portion of fish in the middle of each plate and sprinkle some of the crispy prosciutto on top. Garnish with a small sprig of rosemary on the side.

Veal *straccetti* with sage and culatello di zibello

Straccetti di vitello con salvia e culatello di zibello

An elegant, quick and easy recipe for any occasion.

CUT THE ESCALOPES into 2cm strips and toss in a little flour until they are lightly coated. Shake off any excess flour.

Heat the olive oil in a large pan over a low heat. Sweat the shallot in the oil for about 5 minutes, just until it becomes translucent. Add the sage leaves to the pan and leave for a couple of minutes.

Add the strips of veal and cook for 2 minutes. Stir in the Marsala and increase the heat momentarily to cook off the alcohol. Continue cooking for 1 minute more.

Add the culatello to the saucepan and stir. Season to taste with salt and pepper. Serve on a bed of rocket.

SERVES 4–6

600g thinly sliced escalopes of veal (about 12 slices)
plain flour
4 tablespoons extra virgin olive oil
1 shallot, finely sliced
4 fresh sage leaves
100ml Marsala
6 slices of culatello di zibello or prosciutto, cut into thin strips
salt and freshly ground black pepper
bunch of rocket

I like to cook veal liver in this way and finish it with a little orange zest. Alternatively, you could also use fillet of beef.

Heirloom tomato, rocket and carpaccio of mushroom salad

Insalata di pomodori nostrani, rucola e carpaccio di funghi

You can savour the earthy flavour of mushrooms when eaten raw. In fact, this salad makes a great bruschetta topping, so you might want to make a little extra.

SLICE THE MUSHROOMS wafer thin and toss in 50ml of the oil, the lemon juice and a grinding of black pepper. Place in the fridge for 1 hour.

Toss the tomatoes, rocket and mushrooms with the rest of the olive oil, the balsamic vinegar and a pinch of salt in a large serving bowl. Serve straightaway.

SERVES 4–6

200g champignon or brown cap
   mushrooms, cleaned
100ml extra virgin olive oil
juice of 1 lemon
freshly ground black pepper
200g ripe heirloom tomatoes,
   quartered
100g rocket
20ml balsamic vinegar
salt

Add Pecorino shavings for a nice variation.

Pannacotta with passion fruit coulis

Pannacotta con frutto della passione

Frutto della passione literally translates as fruit of passion – a fitting dessert for a St Valentine's Day feast.

SOAK THE GELATINE in a bowl of water for 10 minutes.

Meanwhile, heat the milk in a small saucepan until it's simmering. Remove the gelatine sheets from the water and stir them into the milk until they dissolve.

Heat the cream in a separate medium saucepan. Stir in the icing sugar until it dissolves. Slice the vanilla pods lengthways and scrape the seeds into the cream. Pour the milk through a strainer into the cream and stir gently.

Pour the pannacotta into 4 x 200ml ramekins and allow to cool. Cover with tin foil and put in the fridge for a couple of hours to set.

To make the passion fruit coulis, cut the passion fruit in half and remove the pulp. Pass the pulp through a sieve into a bowl and save the seeds to use as decoration. Place the strained pulp, icing sugar and orange juice in a small saucepan and simmer for 5 minutes.

To remove the pannacotta from the ramekins, quickly dip each ramekin in hot water to loosen it, but do not let the pannacotta come into contact with the water. Turn out the pannacotta and serve on individual plates. Spoon over some of the passion fruit coulis and decorate with a few passion fruit seeds.

SERVES 4

3 gelatine leaves
150ml fresh milk
1 litre double cream
150g icing sugar
2 vanilla pods

For the passion fruit coulis:
12 passion fruit
150g icing sugar
juice of 1 orange

Pannacotta lends itself to many kinds of coulis, such as the raspberry coulis on page 321.

WOMEN'S DAY MIMOSA DINNER

La Festa della Donna

PRESENT

Large group of female friends

....

ANTIPASTO

Crudités with *pinzimonio* and bagna cauda

PASTA

Orecchiette with broccoli rabe, Italian sausage and fennel fronds
Risotto with smoked salmon, asparagus and lemon

MAINS

Aubergine *parmigiana*

SIDES

Kiwi, pistachio and feta salad

DESSERT

Mimosa cake

LIVING

away from Italy, I really miss *la festa della donna*, a unique occasion for women, young and old, to get together. On the 8th of March, all the restaurants throughout Italy are booked out by gorgeous, vivacious women. Mimosa branches are respectfully gifted to women by menfolk and I can't help but note the similarity to the offering of an olive branch...

While living in Italy, I didn't have much luck with cars – you may remember my New Year's Eve story from page 22. On another occasion, accompanied by my good Mumbian friend Semina, I was driving my very old and much-loved Fiat Bambino, laden down with mimosa for a *festa della donna* dinner, when I inadvertently pulled to a halt at an orange traffic light. The car was forcefully catapulted forward with a huge thud, as a vehicle had driven into the back.

With barely any time to recover from the shock, I was confronted by a hysterical middle-aged, pot-bellied man (greying at the temples, I might add) 'accusing' me of stopping at an orange traffic light. His shirt was far too tight and I found myself staring straight into his hairy navel. He eventually calmed down and assured me that the back of my car was fine – *'non ti preoccupare signorina, la macchina é a posto'* – and took off at great speed.

Needless to say, the car wouldn't start and I innocently presumed I was out of petrol. As luck would have it, this incident occurred on a hill and there was a garage conveniently located at the bottom of the slope. Semina hitched up her traditional sari, pushed us off and we 'drove' into the garage.

I told the attendant that I was experiencing a little trouble, probably engine trouble, and asked if he wouldn't mind checking it out and perhaps filling half the tank with petrol while he was at it. It just wasn't my day, because here was another irate gentleman, this time accusing me of *uno scherzo*, or pulling his leg, saying, 'You foreign women like to joke with the men on Women's Day.' I got out of the car to try to understand the source of the problem and then I saw what it was: there was no engine in the car! We had apparently dropped it back at the stoplight. It was only then that I realised that the engine of the Bambino was located in the rear of the car.

We abandoned the car right there, never to be seen again, unloaded the mimosa and proceeded on foot to the restaurant. I didn't spend much time at the dinner but instead passed the night in the A&E on an intravenous drip of antihistamines. I had had an acute reaction to the mimosa – or was it those men? Funnily enough, after that I swore I would never marry an Italian, but never say never! *Che giornata* – what a day.

Crudités with *pinzimonio* and bagna cauda

Crudités con pinzimonio e bagna cauda

The idea here is to serve raw vegetables for dipping in the two sauces. This appetizer is appropriate for a gathering of friends, dipping and chatting, and since there is so much garlic in the bagna cauda and so much chat going on, you probably won't be kissing anyone anyway!

TO MAKE THE BAGNA CAUDA, heat the butter, oil, anchovies, garlic and a pinch of salt over a low heat, until the butter has melted, the anchovies have dissolved and the garlic has softened. Whisk to combine the butter and oil. Divide the sauce between six warm small dipping bowls.

To make the *pinzimonio*, simply whisk together the oil and vinegar with a pinch of salt and divide the sauce between six small dipping bowls.

Place the raw vegetables decoratively upright in a wide bowl to let everyone help themselves. Each person has two bowls, one of each type of dip.

SERVES 6

8 celery sticks, cleaned and cut into batons
4 red or yellow peppers, cut into strips
4 cucumbers, cut into batons
4 carrots, peeled and cut into batons
2 heads of radicchio, cut into strips

For the bagna cauda:
250g butter
350ml extra virgin olive oil
12 anchovies preserved in oil
4 garlic cloves, thinly sliced
pinch of salt

For the pinzimonio:
250ml good-quality extra virgin olive oil
50ml balsamic vinegar
pinch of salt

Bagna cauda should be served hot or warm, so make it at the last minute. And the nicer the oil, the nicer the pinzimonio. *You can also serve cooked veg such as broccoli or cauliflower florets, cooked just until it's al dente.*

Orecchiette with broccoli rabe, Italian sausage and fennel fronds

Orecchiette con cime di rapa, salsiccia e finocchiona

Orecchiette, a pasta that is widely used in Puglia, has a lovely bite. You can make your own or buy dried or fresh orecchiette. My dearest friend Leonilda, who hails from both Eritrea and Puglia, would whip up this pasta dish for me whenever I had a problem. She always had a solution: 'Let's eat something and talk about it.' While she cooked, she calmed me down and told stories of Eritrea and Ethiopia, imparting ancient philosophies, and everything was just fine.

COOK THE BROCCOLI rabe in a large saucepan of boiling salted water for 30–45 minutes, until tender to the point of being almost overcooked. Drain very well but reserve the cooking water for the pasta. Remove as much liquid as possible and chop roughly.

Put the reserved water in a large saucepan and bring to a boil. Cook the orecchiette in this water for 2–3 minutes if using fresh orecchiette, until they float to the top. If using dried, cook according to the packet instructions.

Continued overleaf

SERVES 6–8

1kg broccoli rabe or turnip tops
500g fresh or dried orecchiette
4 tablespoons extra virgin olive oil
500g fresh Italian salsiccia sausage
150ml dry white wine
small bunch of fennel fronds, finely chopped
salt and freshly ground black pepper
20g freshly grated hard ricotta or Pecorino cheese

Use regular broccoli or Swiss chard if you can't find broccoli rabe and cook it for 10 minutes in boiling salted water.

Heat the olive oil in a large pan over a medium heat. Remove the sausagemeat from its skin and sauté it in the oil for 5 minutes. Add the white wine and increase the heat momentarily to cook off the alcohol. Add the chopped broccoli rabe and the fennel fronds. Season with salt and pepper, but be careful with the salt, as the Pecorino is salty.

Drain the pasta and add it to the pan of sausage and broccoli rabe, tossing everything together. Serve in a large dish with plenty of grated ricotta or Pecorino. Eat immediately.

Risotto with smoked salmon, asparagus and lemon

Risotto con salmone affumicato, asparagi e limone

Being a redheaded teenager in Ireland was no fun. I was teased constantly and called Redser, Rusty, Ginger and Goldilocks, which made me blush from my cheeks right down to my feet. And the more self-conscious I was about it, the hotter and more awkward and unattractive I became. But all that changed when I arrived in Italy. I was told that I had the loveliest blue eyes and golden hair, and the nicest, sweetest voice. Even though there was probably little truth in those compliments, I did relish the overdue attention. Life was dredged of dreariness and replaced with fun, sun and brilliant blue skies.

Back in the mid-1970s, young Italian women were still very much controlled by the *famiglia* (family) and didn't have the freedom to go out and about in the evenings unaccompanied, so foreign girls were a novelty, as we were the only unaccompanied girls about town. Every evening out ended up with a group of admirers vying for telephone numbers. It was all quite innocent and good fun.

As my friends and I strolled along the stands of the Festa di Noantri in Trastevere on one particularly hot summer evening, young enough to giggle over pretty pink candyfloss, caramel-coated hazelnuts and hot roasted peanuts, two flirtatious guys in a Fiat Bambino followed us the full length of the *viale*, driving on the footpath until we relented and agreed to join them for a risotto at Vicolo del Moro. In true Italian courting style, we were taught the essence of a good risotto and learned to sing '*Roma non fa la stupida sta sera*'. Our friend Jill eventually married the driver, Riccardo, who turned out to be a trainee nurse working at the Vatican. He had great perks and we all benefited in some way

SERVES 6

500g asparagus

1 litre cold water

4 tablespoons extra virgin olive oil

4 shallots, finely sliced

2 bay leaves

360g Carnaroli or Vialone Nano rice

500g Irish smoked salmon, chopped

juice and zest of 1 lemon

200ml dry white wine

50g butter

20g freshly grated Pecorino

For the broth:

1 medium onion, peeled and left whole

1 carrot, peeled and left whole

1 celery stick

salt and freshly ground black pepper

or another: private tours of the inner chambers, cheap postage stamps and papal blessings galore for the folks back home.

Smoked salmon always reminded me of home – a lustrous orange reminiscent of Dublin Bay prawns, mussels, Irish red setters, city foxes, flags, Sandymount sunsets and yes, even redheads.

BEND THE ASPARAGUS until it naturally snaps and discard the woody ends. Cook the asparagus in 1 litre of boiling salted water for 2 minutes and remove with a slotted spoon. Chop the cooked asparagus into 2cm pieces and set aside.

To make the broth, add the onion, carrot, celery and a generous seasoning of salt and pepper to the same pot of water that you cooked the asparagus in. Bring to a boil, then reduce the heat and simmer on a low heat for 30 minutes. Remove the vegetables with a slotted spoon and discard them (or you could eat them dressed with a little olive oil). Keep the broth hot.

Heat the olive oil in a large, wide, heavy-based saucepan over a low heat. Sauté the shallots and the bay leaves in the oil for about 5 minutes, until the shallots are soft and translucent. Remove the bay leaves. Add the rice and allow it to absorb the oil in the saucepan for a few minutes, until it turns translucent.

Fold in half of the asparagus, half of the smoked salmon and all of the lemon zest. Pour in the wine and lemon juice and increase the heat momentarily to cook off the alcohol.

Add the hot broth one ladleful at a time. Stir constantly until all the broth has been absorbed before adding the next ladle. Keep adding the broth bit by bit and stirring until all the broth has been absorbed, which should take about 20 minutes.

When the rice is cooked but still has a little bite, fold in the rest of the asparagus and smoked salmon with the butter and Pecorino. Serve immediately with some freshly ground black pepper.

Aubergine *parmigiana*

Melanzane alla parmigiana

I guarantee that this is the best *parmigiana* you will ever have eaten!

To make the tomato sauce, heat the olive oil in a wide, heavy-based saucepan over a low heat. Sweat the shallots for 5 minutes, until they are soft and translucent. Place the tinned tomatoes in a bowl and mash them with a fork. Add the mashed and fresh tomatoes to the saucepan with the basil and salt. Stir, cover and cook for 15 minutes. Blend with a hand blender.

Preheat the oven to 200℃. Lay the slices of aubergine on a baking tray. Sprinkle with coarse salt and leave for 1 hour to extract the bitter juices. Rinse and pat dry.

Place the beaten eggs and the breadcrumbs in two separate shallow bowls. Dip the aubergine slices first in the egg and then the breadcrumbs, shaking off any excess each time.

Heat the oil in a large saucepan or deep-fat fryer until it reaches 165–170℃. Test the oil by dropping in a cube of bread – when the oil is hot enough, it should quickly turn golden. Deep-fry the breaded aubergines until they turn golden. Carefully lift the aubergines out of the oil with a fish slice and rest on kitchen paper to remove the excess oil.

Brush a deep-sided 26cm square baking dish with oil. Line the bottom of the tray with a layer of the breaded aubergines. Spoon over one-quarter of the tomato sauce and sprinkle with one-quarter of the mozzarella and parmigiano and the odd basil leaf. Repeat the layers three more times, finishing with the cheeses.

Bake in the hot oven for 30 minutes. Allow to stand for about 10 minutes before cutting. Cut into 9–12 portions and serve.

Serves 9

4 medium aubergines, sliced
    lengthways 1cm thick
coarse sea salt
4 free-range or organic eggs, beaten
500g Italian dried breadcrumbs
    (pangrattato)
1 litre sunflower or nut oil, for frying
500g buffalo mozzarella, diced and
    drained in a colander or sieve to
    remove excess moisture
200g freshly grated parmigiano
bunch of basil leaves

For the tomato sauce:
4 tablespoons extra virgin olive oil
2 shallots, finely sliced
2 x 400g tins of whole plum tomatoes
2 fresh ripe plum tomatoes, chopped
4 fresh basil leaves
1 teaspoon salt

For a lighter version, do not coat the aubergines in breadcrumbs and chargrill the aubergine slices on a hot griddle pan for 4 minutes on each side instead of frying them.

Kiwi, pistachio and feta salad

Insalata di kiwi, quartirolo e pistacchio

While away the hours on the fabulous floating terrace of La Piscina restaurant on le Zattere in Venice, where you can enjoy a good kiwi salad. Their antipasti are decent, but their calling card is the breathtaking view of the Giudecca Canal, a scene your heart will yearn for and never tire of.

SHRED THE BABY GEM LETTUCE and place in a large serving bowl with the kiwi, feta and pistachios.

Whisk together the olive oil and vinegar in a jug, the pour over the salad. Toss everything together and serve.

SERVES 4–6

300g salad leaves, such as Baby Gem and rocket

4 kiwi, peeled and thinly sliced

200g quartirolo or feta cheese, cut into cubes

25g shelled pistachio nuts

100ml extra virgin olive oil

20ml balsamic vinegar

Replace the kiwi with crisp green apple sliced wafer thin along with toasted pine nuts.

Mimosa cake

La torta mimosa

A fluffy, light yellow cake recalling the delicacy of the mimosa flower.

To MAKE THE SPONGE, preheat the oven to 180℃. Grease two 22cm sponge tins.

Beat together the sugar and the four whole eggs until it's a creamy consistency. Add the egg yolks and continue to beat until they are well incorporated. Add the flour and cornflour and mix until just combined.

Divide the batter between the two greased tins. Bake for 30 minutes, until a skewer inserted into the centre of the cakes comes out clean. Cool on a wire rack, then cut away the crust completely (top and sides) and discard. Cut each sponge in half horizontally so that you have four layers.

Meanwhile, to make the custard, put 300ml of the cream and all of the milk in a medium saucepan. Slice the vanilla pod lengthways and scrape the seeds into the pan. Heat the milk, cream and vanilla to just below the simmering point.

Continued overleaf

SERVES 8

For the sponge:
200g caster sugar
4 free-range or organic eggs
8 free-range or organic egg yolks
200g self-raising flour
40g cornflour, sifted

For the custard cream:
500ml fresh cream
300ml milk
1 vanilla pod
8 free-range or organic egg yolks
200g caster sugar
55g cornflour, sifted
20g icing sugar, sifted

For the syrup:
50g caster sugar
100ml Cointreau orange liqueur
100ml water

In a separate bowl, whisk together the egg yolks, caster sugar and cornflour really well, until thick and pale. Whisk a little of the warm milk into the egg yolk mixture, then slowly pour in the rest, whisking continuously so the eggs don't scramble. Pour the custard back into the saucepan and cook gently over a low heat for a couple of minutes, stirring with a wooden spoon until the custard thickens and coats the back of the spoon. Pour into a bowl and allow to cool, stirring now and then to prevent a skin from forming. Once the custard is cool, whip the remaining 200ml cream and the icing sugar until soft peaks form, then fold into the cooled custard.

To make the syrup, place the sugar, Cointreau and water in a small saucepan. Heat to the simmering point and let it gently bubble away until the sugar has dissolved and it turns thick and syrupy. Set aside to cool.

To assemble, cut one layer of cake into 1cm strips and then cut across to create 1cm cubes. Place the remaining three layers on a wire rack set over a baking tray and dampen with the Cointreau syrup.

Place one sponge cake layer on a serving plate and cover with some of the custard cream. Repeat with the second and third cakes, finishing with a thin layer of custard cream. Make sure you keep back enough custard cream to also decorate the top and sides.

Mix the cake cubes with the remaining custard cream and use this to decorate the top and sides of the cake. Refrigerate for 1 or 2 hours to allow the custard cream to set a little.

FATHER'S DAY

La Festa del Papá

PRESENT

The family

....

ANTIPASTO

Bruschetta with burrata, wilted radicchio,
toasted pine nuts and balsamic reduction

PASTA

Schiaffoni with wild hare

RISOTTO

Risotto with radicchio, pancetta and Barbera

MAINS

Stuffed courgettes

SIDES

Balsamic and garlic French beans

DESSERT

Giorgio's coffee granita
Custard fritters

FATHER'S Day coincides with the feast of the national patron saint, San Giuseppe, or Saint Joseph,

the carpenter. The *festa* occurs during Lent, a time of fasting prior to Easter for practising Catholics. Traditionally no meat was eaten during Lent and the Father's Day dinner was a solemn affair. Nowadays, though, Father's Day is enjoyed very much, just as Hallmark predicted, and I suggest a more masculine-themed dinner.

During my early years in Italy I was fascinated by these large family affairs and I loved being invited. Italians are a generous people and there is always room at the table for one more. One fond memory relates to the time my newly acquired friend invited me to her house for Father's Day dinner. Her *papá*, very much the man of the house, asked me what winters are like in Ireland. I had been talking with my father that very same morning about a freak snow storm back home, and delighted to have a chance to practise my Italian, I confidently told Signor Bianchi, 'I have snow on my tits today.' You see, *tetti* is roofs and *tette* is tits! Putting the sudden silence in the room down to my riveting conversation, I carried on, describing how my father likes to make jam without condoms, *senza preservative*. *Preservativi* is condoms, whereas I of course meant without preservatives. I was trying hard to impress him, knowing how much Italians like natural, homemade foods!

Every dinner ended the same way, with someone shaking their head and saying '*quella straniera*' (that foreigner), meaning I just wasn't the same as Italian women; there was something odd about me. But I like to think I was referred to as *quella straniera* with a touch of tenderness. After all, there was so much for me to learn, and so many teachers eager to intervene.

Bruschetta with burrata, wilted radicchio, toasted pine nuts and balsamic reduction

Bruschetta con burrata, radicchio, pinoli tostati e riduzione di balsamico

Creamy burrata and bitter radicchio contrast beautifully and bond gracefully with sweet balsamic and toasted pine nuts.

FIRST MAKE THE BALSAMIC REDUCTION. Place the vinegar in a small heavy-based saucepan over a low heat. Cook gently for about 20 minutes, until it has reduced by two-thirds. Set aside for 1 hour or so.

Place the radicchio leaves on a hot griddle pan and turn them over several times, just until the leaves are charred and wilted but not burned. Chop roughly and leave to cool. If using the long-leafed variety of radicchio, keep the leaves whole and use two leaves per bruschetta.

Toast the pine nuts on a hot, dry pan for 30 seconds, taking care not to let them burn.

Working in batches, toast the baguette slices on both sides on the griddle pan. While the bread is still hot, drizzle with a little olive oil.

Place some wilted radicchio on each slice of bread, followed by some torn burrata. Sprinkle with toasted pine nuts and lightly drizzle over the balsamic reduction and some honey.

To serve, place some fresh radicchio leaves on a large plate and place the bruschette decoratively on top.

MAKES 12

250ml balsamic vinegar
2 tablespoons honey
1 head of radicchio (set some leaves aside for garnish)
30g pine nuts
1 or 2 baguettes (enough for 12 x 2cm slices)
good-quality extra virgin olive oil
500g fresh burrata, torn into shreds (or use creamy goat's cheese or buffalo mozzarella)

Schiaffoni with wild hare

Schiaffoni al sugo di lepre

Schiaffoni is a very satisfying pasta and one of my favourites. Large and silky, it contains the sauce and hare meat perfectly. Traditionally, wild hare is marinated and stewed with its own blood and offal. Realistically, you will be using a farmed hare, so this recipe is adapted to modern city living.

PLACE THE HARE PIECES IN A BOWL and pour in enough wine to cover them. Add the rest of the marinade ingredients. Cover and place in the fridge for at least 12 hours or overnight. Remove the hare from the marinade and reserve it for the sauce. Pat the hare dry with kitchen paper and coat lightly in flour.

Heat the olive oil in a large saucepan over a low heat. Gently sauté the garlic and anchovies, if using, for about 1 minute, just until the garlic is fragrant but not browned. Stir in the chilli flakes, then add in the hare pieces and brown them all over. Pour in the marinade and increase the heat momentarily to cook off the alcohol in the wine.

Place the tomatoes in a bowl and mash them with a fork, then add them to the saucepan. Cover and cook for 1 hour, until the meat comes away easily from the bone. Add a little warm water if the sauce looks too dry.

Remove the hare pieces with a slotted spoon and separate the meat from the bones. Stir the lemon zest into the sauce, if using, then add the meat back in.

Cook the pasta in a large saucepan of boiling salted water until al dente or according to the packet instructions. Drain and add to the saucepan, stirring to coat the pasta in the sauce. Tip onto a large serving platter, garnish with the parsley and serve immediately.

SERVES 6–8

1 hare, skinned, cleaned, and cut into 8 pieces
plain flour, for coating
4 tablespoons extra virgin olive oil
2 garlic cloves, crushed
3 salted anchovies (optional)
1 tablespoon dried chilli flakes
2 x 400g tins of whole plum tomatoes
zest of ½ lemon (optional)
500g schiaffoni pasta or pappardelle
2 tablespoons chopped fresh flat-leaf parsley

For the marinade:

500ml red wine or enough to cover the hare completely in a bowl
6 bay leaves
6 fresh sage leaves
small sprig of fresh rosemary
small sprig of fresh thyme
2 tablespoons juniper berries
1 tablespoon salt
freshly ground black pepper

Risotto with radicchio, pancetta and Barbera

Risotto con radicchio, pancetta e barbera

As an importer, I have access to the very best Italian wines. Meeting the people behind the wines, learning their stories and appreciating the sheer hard work it takes to produce great wine is an enormous privilege. And yet during all the years that I have lived in and travelled throughout Italy, I have rarely indulged in a truly nice wine when invited to someone's home for dinner. Great fanfare is involved in presenting the wine at the table. The man of the house announces, 'This is the best wine you have ever tasted, made by my *nonno* (grandfather), *zio* (uncle), *cugino* (cousin) or the local *contadino* (farmer) who makes it for himself and gives it to nobody else except me.' The initial introduction is followed by a series of adjectives such as *genuino* (genuine), *naturale* (natural), *storico* (historical) or *tradizionale* (traditional). In reality, this translates into a wine that is homemade, awful and laced with sulphites and that needs some hefty food to absorb the overpowering tannins. At the same time, though, those are also the most memorable dinners. There is always a recipe to take away, a story to be passed on and new friendships to be formed. Maybe that wine wasn't so bad after all.

TO MAKE THE BROTH, fill a saucepan with 1 litre of cold water and add in the vegetables and a generous seasoning of salt and pepper. Bring to a boil, then reduce the heat to low and simmer for 30 minutes. Remove the vegetables with a slotted spoon and discard them (or you could eat them dressed with a little olive oil). Keep the broth hot.

Continued overleaf

SERVES 6

4 tablespoons extra virgin olive oil
2 shallots, finely sliced
200g pancetta, finely sliced and cut into thin strips
360g Carnaroli, Vialone Nano or Arborio rice
1 medium head of radicchio, leaves separated and shredded
500ml Barbera red wine
salt and freshly ground black pepper
50g butter
50g freshly grated parmigiano

For the broth:
1 litre cold water
1 medium onion, peeled and left whole
1 carrot, peeled and left whole
1 celery stick
salt and freshly ground black pepper

OMA

12 litografie
riprodotte da disegni originali
di

Antonio Carbonati

Heat the oil in a large, wide, heavy-based saucepan over a low heat. Sweat the shallots in the oil for about 5 minutes, until they are soft and translucent. Add the pancetta and cook for about 2 minutes, until it turns a nice deep pink colour. Add the rice and allow it to absorb the oil in the saucepan for a couple of minutes, until it starts to turn translucent.

Add half of the radicchio and stir until it wilts. Pour in half of the wine and increase the heat momentarily to cook off the alcohol.

Add the hot broth one ladleful at a time. Stir constantly until all the broth has been absorbed before adding the next ladle. Keep adding the broth bit by bit and stirring until all the broth has been absorbed, which should take about 20 minutes.

Pour in the rest of the wine a little at a time, continuing to stir for another 5 minutes. Fold in the rest of the radicchio. Season with salt and pepper, then stir in the butter and half of the parmigiano.

Tip the risotto into a serving bowl, sprinkle with the rest of the parmigiano and serve immediately.

You can serve this risotto in a large radicchio leaf, which enhances the striking red colour of the risotto.

Stuffed courgettes

Zucchini ripieni (alla romana)

The best *zucchini ripiene alla romana* I have ever had were served in a very small coffee bar, The Golden Bar, on the busy Cristoforo Colombo. It was where my friend Semina and I had our weekly Thursday lunch treat of stuffed courgettes in a homely tomato sauce, with a fresh rosetta bread roll and half a glass of Montepulciano wine. As we diligently filed away the confidential records of UN staff, we looked forward to that lunch all week, wondering if the stuffing and sauce would be as good as it had been the week before and hoping our seats by the window would be free, next to the stern elderly gentleman who sat reading his *La Repubblica* newspaper, with his cane, hat and cashmere coat dangling from the sole peg on the yellow smoke-stained wall. Giovanni, the barista, would greet us with a welcoming shout that ricocheted across the room when he spied us at the door: '*Ciao bellissimi, la vostra tavola é pronta!*' (Hello beautifuls, your table is ready!)

TO MAKE THE SAUCE, you'll need a saucepan that is wide enough to fit six courgettes horizontally. Heat the olive oil in the pan over a medium heat. Sweat the onion and rosemary for 5 minutes, then remove the rosemary. Place the tomatoes in a bowl and mash them with a fork, then add to the pan along with the warm water and salt and cook for 5 minutes more. Remove the pan from the heat while you prepare the stuffing.

Continued overleaf

SERVES 6

300g finely minced beef or lamb

50g fresh breadcrumbs

20g freshly grated parmigiano

20g pine nuts

1 shallot, finely diced

1 free-range or organic egg yolk, beaten

zest of 1 lemon

pinch of salt

6 medium courgettes

2 tablespoons extra virgin olive oil

For the tomato sauce:

4 tablespoons extra virgin olive oil

1 medium onion, finely sliced

small sprig of fresh rosemary

2 x 400g tins of whole plum tomatoes

50ml warm water

1 teaspoon salt

Combine the minced meat, breadcrumbs, parmigiano, pine nuts, shallot, egg yolk, lemon zest and a pinch of salt in a large bowl. Mix well, until smooth.

Trim the ends from the courgettes. Using a corer, remove the centre of each courgette and fill with the stuffing.

Heat 2 tablespoons of olive oil in another large saucepan over a medium heat. Lightly brown the courgettes all over. Gently lift them from the saucepan and lay them in the bottom of the saucepan with the sauce. Return the saucepan to a low heat, cover and cook for 40 minutes, until the meat is cooked through and the courgettes are tender. Serve a whole stuffed courgette per person and spoon over the sauce. Delicious with thick slices of toasted crusty bread.

Balsamic and garlic French beans

Fagiolini con aglio e aceto balsamico di Modena

The problem with these beans is that they are so good, my vegetarian daughter, Federica, and I start to eat them in the kitchen before they ever arrive to the table. We scold each other and laugh, knowing what Stefano will say with a dramatic hand movement and a sigh of indignation: '*Ma, che fine hanno fatto i fagiolini?*' (But what happened to the string beans?) Make a double batch.

COOK THE FRENCH BEANS in boiling salted water for 10 minutes. Drain and place in a serving dish.

Shake the oil, vinegar, garlic and some salt and pepper in a screw-top jar until well combined. Pour over the beans, mix well and serve while hot.

SERVES 6–8

1kg French beans
50ml extra virgin olive oil
50ml good-quality balsamic
   vinegar
2 garlic cloves, thinly sliced
salt and freshly ground black
   pepper

Giorgio's coffee granita

Il granita di caffé di Giorgio

My father-in-law, Giorgio, managed to make the granita in silence and secrecy, a seductive process that started at 5am in the morning. He was a small, handsome man of few words, always immersed in his books, guided by an enormous magnifying glass. He enjoyed company and his two allotted jobs: making the *granita di caffé* and filling the dishwasher after dinner. He spent a lot of time on both exercises, precision and order being the essence of perfection.

SWEETEN THE HOT COFFEE with the caster sugar. Allow to cool, then pour into a shallow baking tray and place in the freezer.

Remove from the freezer after 30 minutes – it should be only partially frozen. Using a whisk or fork, break it up and return the tray to the freezer. Repeat this process six to eight times, until small icicles have formed.

In the meantime, whisk together the cream and icing sugar until the cream has been whipped to the soft peak stage.

To prepare the granita, place a tablespoon of whipped cream in the bottom of ice cream soda glasses. Add a couple tablespoons of coffee granita and continue to layer it up, finishing with a dollop of cream and a sprig of fresh mint.

SERVES 6–8

1 litre strong, hot black coffee (or 6 espressos topped up with hot water to make 1 litre)
300g caster sugar
250ml double cream
300g icing sugar, sifted
fresh mint sprigs, to decorate

Custard fritters

Zeppole di San Giuseppe

The *festa* of *San Giuseppe il patrono*, St Joseph the patron saint, is a significant festival in southern Italy. Religious processions parading huge Fellini-esque statues of Giuseppe and the Madonna (think of the film *Roma*) through towns lined with stalls tempting the soul with earthly pleasures are commonplace.

The utterly scrumptious *zeppole di San Giuseppe* only appear in the pastry shops for a couple of days at this time of the year. I tend to buy a tray each day, and as I munch through the crispy pastry, my tears mix with the fragrant vanilla custard at the thought of having to wait another year to eat them again. Of course, that's not true. While I would love to have *zeppole* any time of year, the suspense of having to wait for them is a little thrilling. Croissants, buns and *bignè* are moved backstage to the bar counter and the *zeppole* are piled high in the windows to announce the feast of San Giuseppe.

To make the custard, put the milk in a medium saucepan. Slice the vanilla pod lengthways and scrape the seeds into the milk. Warm the milk over a low heat.

In a separate bowl, whisk together the egg yolks, sugar and cornflour really well, until thick and creamy. Whisk a little of the warm milk into the egg yolk mixture, then slowly pour in the rest, whisking continuously so the eggs don't scramble. Pour the custard back into the saucepan and cook gently over a low heat for a couple of minutes, stirring with a wooden spoon until the custard thickens. Pour into a jug and cover with cling film to prevent a skin from forming.

MAKES 9

70g butter

250ml water

140g plain flour

40g caster sugar

3 free-range or organic eggs, beaten

zest of 1 lemon

1 litre sunflower oil, for deep-frying

fresh raspberries, strawberries or glacé cherries, to decorate

For the custard:

250ml milk

1 vanilla pod

3 free-range or organic egg yolks, beaten

75g caster sugar

25g cornflour, sifted

To make the pastry, place the butter and water in a medium-sized heavy-based saucepan and bring to the simmering point. Allow the butter to melt while you stir with a wooden spoon. Remove the saucepan from the heat and sift in the flour. Return the saucepan to the heat and mix the ingredients together well to form a pastry.

Transfer the pastry to a mixing bowl and add the sugar, beaten eggs and lemon zest, mixing vigorously until it's all incorporated. Place in a pastry bag fitted with a star nozzle.

Cut some parchment paper into 8cm squares. Pipe little 6cm nests onto the centre of each square.

Heat the sunflower oil in a deep saucepan or deep-fat fryer to 165°C. Pop a couple of *zeppole* into the oil, paper and all. When the paper floats to the top, remove and discard it. Fry the *zeppole* for a couple of minutes, until golden, and remove with a slotted spoon. Place on a tray lined with kitchen paper to absorb the excess oil and leave to cool.

Fill the centre of each *zeppole* with custard. Decorate with a raspberry, strawberry or half a glacé cherry.

EASTER SUNDAY AND MONDAY LUNCH

Il Pranzo di Pasqua e Pasquetta

PRESENT

Family and friends

ANTIPASTO

Lamb and artichoke *coratella*

PASTA

Crespelle with smoked mozzarella and broccoli

MAINS

Grilled lamb chops with mint pesto

SIDES

Roast potatoes, peppers and black olives

DESSERT

Dark chocolate Neapolitan *pastiera* cake

ONE DAY out of the blue we received an invitation from my husband's posh aunt to partake in a traditional family Easter lunch at her English-style villa. Aunt Luisa had a formidable reputation for chasing away daughters-in-law; both her sons had married several times. I was expecting my second child and was delighted to sit next to another *straniera* (foreigner), a beautiful Norwegian woman, the cousin's third wife and mother of the only granddaughter. She spent the entire lunch warning me about Italian mothers-in-law. 'You know, you will only be a surrogate mother to this child – that child is for *them*,' she spat. Mind you, by this point she had consumed a considerable amount of white wine. In the background I could hear echoes bounce from one end of the table to the other: '*Di che cosa parlano loro due?*' (What are they talking about?)

That evening, back in the comfort of my own home, I said, 'I have no intention of being a surrogate mother to this child. He's mine – all mine.' Stefano thought I'd gone insane. He put it down to the hormones and tried to calm me with some insipid camomile tea. Just as we Irish cure all ailments with a cup of tea, the Italians hold the same faith in camomile.

I gave birth on a beautiful day in April to my second son, Sean. I had barely recovered from the labour when a troupe arrived at my bedside consisting of mother-in-law, sisters-in-law and aunts. 'Do you have milk?' they cried out in unison. 'No, she doesn't have milk yet.' 'Put a warm, damp cloth on her breasts.' 'Rub her breasts with olive oil.' 'Only extra virgin – cold pressed works best.' Phone calls were made to every town in Italy to tell the relatives that the first grandson had been born, but unfortunately the *straniera* mother had no milk. 'These *straniere* mothers, what can you expect? They give their babies bottles for generations, now their breasts are redundant.'

Solutions consisting of potions and compounds were delivered liberally. There was no escape, as I was bed bound. Finally, a nurse brought in my son for feeding, and as I stretched to take him, two large hands appeared from nowhere, grabbed my left breast, squeezed my nipple between a thumb and index finger and with the other large hand placed behind my son's head, tried to force my nipple into the baby's mouth. I bawled, the baby bawled and they all looked on, astonished. 'The *straniera* is depressed!' Next ensued the cures for depression: camomile tea, eight cups a day. Not the bought type, but Alberto's camomile picked fresh from his garden. A sister was designated to go and collect the precious flowers while the calls to the *parenti* (relatives) all over Italy started all over again.

I survived well enough to be dispatched home, but I wasn't a wet day home when the entourage returned. During the process of changing Sean's nappy, I was encircled by my mother-in-law, two sisters-in-law and an aunt. They eerily and quietly observed as I nervously removed the soiled nappy. Suddenly, it was grabbed from my hands and passed from one to the other. '*É oro, é oro!*' they shouted. (It's gold, it's gold!) 'Let me see, give it to me. It's true! It's gold, it's gold!'

So you see, if Italian mothers think that their boys shit gold, no wonder Italian men think that they can lay golden eggs!

Lamb and artichoke *coratella*

Coratella finta

Coratella, once the preferred Easter breakfast of Romans, consists of stewed diced mutton, liver, heart, kidney and all the rest, and it's simply delicious. My children, unlike their mother, are reticent about eating offal in any shape or form, so I tend to make a simpler *coratella* to ensure the doves remain flying overhead. I call it *coratella finta* (false or pretend *coratella*).

At L'Uliveto restaurant in the small town of Cineto Romano, Lazio dishes up the most wonderful *coratella*. If you are driving to the Tivoli gardens, Abruzzo or Marche, a pit stop is worthwhile. The terrace offers a spectacular silhouette mountain view and the *lasagnette* with *funghi porcini* (thick spelt fettuccini with fresh porcini mushrooms) are equally good. I feel obliged to mention that Marcello, the owner, is a distant cousin of Stefano's. We had our wedding dinner here, drowned in Marcello's marvellous olive oil and red wine, and danced the tarantella.

CUT 3CM OFF THE TOP OF THE ARTICHOKES and discard. Cut the stem down to 3cm and pare away the outer skin. Remove the outer leaves – the more, the better – leaving only the tender heart of the artichoke. Remove the fuzzy beards, then thinly slice the artichoke hearts. Place in a bowl of water with half a lemon to avoid discolouration.

Heat the olive oil in a large saucepan over a low heat. Sauté the onion, carrot, celery, garlic and bay leaves for 5 minutes, until the onion softens. Add the mince and stir until it takes on a deep pink colour, but do not brown it. Add the artichokes. Pour in the wine and increase the heat momentarily to cook off the alcohol, then stir in the water and some salt and pepper. Cover and cook for 1 hour on a low heat, until the sauce is dense and aromatic. Add a little more water if the sauce becomes dry. Season with salt and pepper to taste. Spoon portions onto radicchio leaves and serve with breadsticks.

SERVES 6

2 artichokes
½ lemon
2 tablespoons extra virgin olive oil
1 red onion, finely diced
1 carrot, finely diced
1 celery stick, finely diced
2 garlic cloves, sliced
2 bay leaves
500g finely minced lamb
200ml white wine
250ml water
salt and freshly ground black
  pepper
1 head of radicchio, leaves
  separated
breadsticks, to serve

Crespelle with smoked mozzarella and broccoli

Crespelle con mozzarella affumicata e broccoli

The first time I had these *crespelle* was in a classy restaurant called Eucalipto on the ancient Roman Via Ardeatina. Classy restaurants tended to have a French flair to them, setting them apart from the much-loved *trattorie*. Wines were decanted, *amuse-bouches* and *petit fours* were presented and a hefty bill came at the end of the meal.

While I was working as a trainee HR assistant at the United Nations offices nearby, my boss, an exceedingly intelligent and sophisticated Sri Lankan lady named Sue, invited her team for a get-together dinner at Eucalipto. There was a blazing fire, wine flowed freely and the conversation was riveting, as our team was comprised of twelve different nationalities. Sue adored her lovable mongrel Bishram and she recounted how Bishram slept on the end of her bed and that she wouldn't have it any other way. Carried away with the merriment of the occasion, I cheekily asked if she gave the dog a bidet each night prior to going to bed. Needless to say, I wasn't in line for a promotion for a very long time.

I would often dream of these *crespelle*, so much so that my first wedding dinner was in that very same restaurant and everyone talked about the *crespelle* for weeks afterwards.

To make the crêpes, whisk together the eggs, milk and some salt and pepper in a medium-sized bowl. Gradually add the flour and keeping whisking until you have a smooth batter. Refrigerate for 30 minutes.

MAKES 8

For the crêpes:
2 free-range or organic eggs, beaten
300ml milk
salt and freshly ground black pepper
150g plain flour
knob of butter

For the béchamel sauce:
25g butter
25g plain flour
250ml milk

For the filling:
250g broccoli florets
25g butter
250g smoked mozzarella, diced

For the topping:
100ml tomato passata
50g freshly grated parmigiano

Remove from the fridge and stir the batter. Melt a knob of butter in a non-stick frying pan (a 22cm pan is ideal). Once the butter is foaming, pour in a half-ladle of the batter and swirl it around to coat the bottom of the pan. Leave it to set for a couple minutes and flip the pancake. Cook the other side for 2 or 3 minutes. Continue until you have made eight pancakes, stacking them between layers of parchment paper as you go.

To make the béchamel, melt the butter in a saucepan. Stirring continuously with a wooden spoon, work in the flour little by little until it has all been absorbed by the butter. Gradually pour in the milk, stirring continuously until all of the milk has been absorbed and the sauce has thickened and coats the back of the spoon.

To make the filling, cook the broccoli in boiling salted water for 5 minutes, just until it's al dente. Drain the broccoli well and plunge into a bowl of ice water to stop it cooking and to keep the vibrant green colour. Melt the butter in a saucepan over a low heat. Add the broccoli and diced mozzarella and stir. Remove from the heat and fold in a couple of spoons of béchamel sauce.

To put it all together, preheat the oven to 200°C. Grease a large rectangular oven dish.

Spread some of the filling over each pancake, leaving a 2cm border. Fold each pancake in half and then in half again. Arrange the pancakes in the greased oven dish by laying them one next to the other. Pour over the rest of the béchamel sauce and drizzle with a little tomato passata. Sprinkle generously with freshly grated parmigiano.

Bake in the oven for 10 minutes, until the parmigiano is golden and the sauce is bubbling. Leave to stand for a couple of minutes, until the sauce stops bubbling. Serve two *crespelle* per person in warm pasta bowls and spoon over the creamy sauce.

Crespelle may seem complicated, but once you make them a couple of times, the process becomes very easy and you can let your imagination run wild. Why not try a truffled mushroom filling? Pan-fry some sliced mushrooms in a little garlic, add a couple drops of truffle oil, fold in the béchamel and assemble as outlined.

Grilled lamb chops with mint pesto

Costolette di agnello con pesto di menta

Easter and lamb are inseparable. Lamb prices soar at this time of year in Italy and your butcher is doing you a favour by even accepting your order. Everyone is talking about lamb: where to buy it, how to cook it, which restaurant serves the best. And note that restaurants are fully booked on Easter Sunday. It's either a day when the whole family (and I mean family and extended family and friends) books a table at a restaurant weeks in advance or there is a huge family gathering at some relative's house.

We usually spend Easter with family and friends in the Marche. I have quite a few Irish friends living in Italy, married to Italians, and we catch up regularly. Our husbands are great friends and I love our special get togethers, which inevitably consist of numerous dinners. Last year we booked our Easter lunch at the local hotel, where we know the chef and appreciate his talents, and the maître d', Piero, has a soft spot for us. As it turned out, there was a set menu and the restaurant was full of local people all dressed in their best clothes, most likely purchased at Mr Buschi's shop in the village. The set menu included as much wine as you liked, crisp white Pecorino or fruity red Montepulciano. As I glanced around the other tables I saw that the wine had barely been touched, whereas I dare not divulge just how many bottles were nestled in front of us. Next year Piero needs to specify 'Easter lunch, chef's set menu, wine included (for Italians only)'.

Continued overleaf

SERVES 4–6

12 lamb chops
100ml extra virgin olive oil
4 garlic cloves, sliced
zest and juice of 1 lemon
freshly ground black pepper

For the mint pesto:
bunch of fresh mint
2 garlic cloves, peeled
200ml extra virgin olive oil
50g freshly grated parmigiano or
    Pecorino
good pinch of salt

WRAP THE CHOPS IN CLING FILM and pound them until they are 1cm thick. Trim off the excess fat and place in a large casserole dish.

Whisk together the olive oil, garlic, lemon zest and juice and a generous seasoning of freshly ground black pepper. Pour the marinade over the chops, cover with cling film and leave in the fridge for a couple of hours.

While the lamb is marinating, make the mint pesto by whizzing all the ingredients in a blender until smooth.

Heat a griddle pan until it's smoking hot. Shake the excess marinade off the lamb chops and cook in batches for 3 minutes on each side. Transfer to a warm plate.

Serve two or three lamb chops per person with a good dollop of mint pesto.

I also like to serve lamb with rocket pesto, as the bitterness of the rocket cuts through the fatty lamb nicely. To make a rocket pesto, just use fresh rocket in place of the mint.

Roast potatoes, peppers and black olives

Patate arrosto con peperoni e olive nere

Il pranzo della domenica (Sunday lunch) is another must-do lunch for Italian families. Grandparents, parents, children and grandchildren come together for a long, reposing meal. While Italian cooking is so diverse from region to region, Sunday lunch tends to be traditional throughout Italy: lasagna, roast lamb and roast potatoes followed by tiramisù or *mignon* pastries. As a working mum I looked forward to the rosemary roast potatoes on Sundays when we strolled over to Stefano's parents' house. The children were indulged, lunch was served on beautiful crockery and we sunk into the velvet settee to watch an old De Sica movie.

PREHEAT THE OVEN to 250℃.

Cut the potatoes in half. Cut the peppers into 6cm x 2cm strips.

Place the potatoes, peppers, olives, garlic and the sprig of rosemary into a large roasting tin. Pour over the olive oil and sprinkle with the salt. Mix well so that everything is coated in the oil.

Roast in the hot oven for 45 minutes, stirring now and then. When roasted, transfer to a serving dish.

SERVES 6–8

1kg baby new potatoes, unpeeled and washed
1 medium red pepper
1 medium yellow pepper
100g black olives
8 garlic cloves, unpeeled and left whole
large sprig of fresh rosemary
200ml extra virgin olive oil
1 tablespoon coarse sea salt

You can add all sorts of ingredients to your potatoes. Try thick carrot or parsnip batons or different herbs, such as thyme, tarragon or a couple of bay leaves.

Dark chocolate Neapolitan *pastiera* cake

La pastiera napoletana

'*A'pastier e' gran*', the cry of street vendors, can be heard resonating among the small back streets of Naples at Easter. Coffee bars and pastry shops challengingly display their *pastiera* cakes and each outlet and Neapolitan family guards their recipes like secret treasure troves.

I dare not mention this to anyone from Parthenope for fear of the *malocchio* (evil eye), but *pastiera* is very similar to the *budino* rice cake on page 42 except that it uses grain instead of rice. This is another traditional Neapolitan recipe from my good friend Giuseppina Energe. It was quite an ordeal getting this recipe from her. It was like extracting gold from a rock. After all, it's the *ricetta di famiglia* (family recipe) and she feared the wrath of family members for divulging their secrets. I promised her I would change it, so I have added dark chocolate, which I feel adds a little luxury to the cake.

To make the pastry, cream the butter, sugar and lemon zest together until pale and fluffy. Add in the eggs one at a time, mixing well. Mix in the flour, then turn out onto a lightly floured board and knead lightly to form a soft dough. Wrap in cling film and place in the fridge for at least 2 hours.

Preheat the oven to 175℃.

SERVES 12

For the pastry:
200g butter, softened
200g caster sugar
zest of 1 lemon
2 free-range or organic eggs, beaten
400g plain flour

For the filling:
500g fresh ricotta
1 x 400g jar of cooked buckwheat grain (*grano*) (available from a good deli)
100g good-quality dark chocolate (at least 75% cocoa solids), chopped
50ml rosewater
5 free-range or organic eggs, beaten
1 vanilla pod

Remove the pastry from the fridge and cut into two pieces in the ratio of two-thirds to one-third. Roll out the larger piece of pastry. Line the base and sides of a 30cm pie dish with the pastry and prick it all over with a fork. You can blind bake the pastry if you wish, but it's not really necessary. If you do want to blind bake it, cover with parchment paper and fill with dried beans. Bake for 15 minutes, then remove the beans and the paper, return the pastry to the oven and bake for 5 minutes more to crisp it up. Set aside to cool while you make the filling.

Mix together the ricotta, cooked grain, chocolate, rosewater and the beaten eggs in a large mixing bowl. Cut the vanilla pod in half lengthways, scrape the seeds into the bowl and mix again.

Pour the filling into the lined pie dish. Roll out the rest of the pastry and cut into long 2cm-wide strips. Lay the strips over the tart to create a lattice effect.

Bake in the oven for about 1 hour, until the pastry is golden and the grain has set. Leave to cool before cutting. This is best served chilled.

We Dubliners love ports, and I can spend hours watching enormous ships, cruisers, yachts and simple wooden boats coming and going from Naples to Capri, Ischia and Procida, offloading their eclectic groups of passengers, each hiding their own personal story. Life unfolds very unexpectedly in this part of the world. We like to stay at the Grand Hotel Vesuvio in Naples, and while it sounds quite grand, the atmosphere is actually pretty laid back. The views from the bedrooms offer unique vistas over the Bay of Naples to the distant and threatening volcano of Vesuvio. A short stroll takes you from the waterfront to Piazza del Plebiscito for thick, syrupy coffee at the iconic Gambrinus bar. Spaghetti alla scialuppa at the restaurant La Scialuppa and the best pizza in the world at Da Michele are worth the trip from anywhere in the world.

MOTHER'S DAY

La Festa della Mamma

PRESENT

Family

....

ANTIPASTO

Fontina cheese and ham strudel

PASTA

Sardinian bottarga tonnarelli

Gnocchetti with chantarelle mushrooms and sun-dried tomatoes

MAINS

Calabrese swordfish *pizzaiola*

Tomatoes stuffed with saffron rice

SIDES

Romanesco broccoli and anchovies

DESSERT

Marsala plums with whipped cream

AN OLD Italian saying is *chi ha la mamma non trema* – who has a mother doesn't tremor (has no fear). Notwithstanding the notoriety attached to the figure of the Italian *mamma, la festa della mamma* is not an important Italian *festa*.

As a young *nuora* (daughter-in-law), I was referred to as the *straniera* (foreigner) and apparently I couldn't do things quite like Italian women. My floors were *unto* (greasy), my daughter caught chickenpox from a draught because I left the window open and my children have flat feet because I let them go barefoot and didn't buy shoes until they could walk. Nevertheless, my in-laws and I grew fond of each other. I miss them dearly and appreciate all of the wonderful recipes, cooking skills and traditions I inherited from them, including how to keep marble floors pristine with a brilliant sheen.

Fontina cheese and ham strudel

Strudel di fontina e prosciutto cotto

A quick and easy puff pastry sandwich that is perfect for brunch or for an *aperitivo*.

PREHEAT THE OVEN to 185°C. Line two baking trays with parchment paper.

Roll out the pastry on a lightly floured board and cut into six equal rectangles.

Place alternate layers of cheese and ham (you want four layers in total) on one half of each rectangle, leaving a 1cm border. Fold over the other half of the rectangle and seal the edges together, crimping with the tines of a fork. Glaze the top of each parcel with a little beaten egg yolk. Transfer to the lined baking trays.

Cook for 20 minutes, until the pastry is golden. Serve warm with a side salad of lightly dressed rocket leaves.

SERVES 6

300g ready-made frozen puff pastry, defrosted and ready to use

500g Fontina cheese, sliced

250g good-quality cooked ham, sliced

1 free-range or organic egg yolk, beaten

lightly dressed rocket leaves, to serve

Sardinian bottarga tonnarelli

Tonnarelli con bottarga

Bottarga is dried fish roe and it is widely used in Sardinian coastal dishes. Roe from the mullet (or tuna, in the case of Sicilian bottarga) are dried and the final product looks like a dark brown rectangular block. The fishy taste is very particular, so it's best used sparingly. Bottarga is delicious grated on pasta – simply use as you need it and pop the block back into the fridge.

COOK THE SPAGHETTI in a large saucepan of boiling salted water until al dente or according to the packet instructions.

Heat the olive oil in a large pan over a low heat. Sauté the anchovies and garlic for about 1 minute, just until the garlic is fragrant but not browned. Blend the anchovies into the oil with a wooden spoon until they dissolve, then stir in the chilli flakes.

Stir in the grated bottarga, then pour in the wine. Increase the heat momentarily to cook off the alcohol. Remove the garlic with a slotted spoon.

Drain the pasta and add it to the pan along with the chopped parsley. Mix everything together well and serve immediately.

SERVES 6

500g tonnarelli egg pasta

4 tablespoons extra virgin olive oil

4 salted anchovies

2 garlic cloves, peeled and left whole

½ teaspoon dried chilli flakes

1 heaped tablespoon grated dried Sardinian bottarga

100ml white wine

2 tablespoons chopped fresh flat-leaf parsley

Bottarga is delicious grated directly on pasta, just like parmigiano, or used instead of anchovies in a soffritto, *although anchovies are significantly cheaper.*

Gnocchetti with chantarelle mushrooms and sun-dried tomatoes

Gnocchetti con finferli e pomodorini secchi

Italian city dwellers tend to combine picnicking with foraging, but foraging is an integral part of the lives of country folk. In the alpine areas such as Trentino, the local authorities have created a foragers' paradise by providing accommodation huts on the mountainsides for communal use. There are strict rules that locals tend to respect, such as brushing off spores before harvesting mushrooms and keeping the huts spick and span.

Zio Mario, a forager and gourmand with a penchant for porcini mushrooms, would take his nieces foraging for mushrooms in the woods around Lake Bracciano. The mushrooms were carefully stored in baskets and taken to the Mercati Generali, the city fruit and vegetable market on the Via Ostiense, where a conscientious mushroom inspector would diligently separate the rogues from the gems. Arriving home that evening with a *fame da lupo* (hunger of a wolf), my aunt Jean would have the gnocchetti laid out like big white pearls on a starched linen cloth. Mario took his place in front of the cooker with due ceremony and we all enjoyed a great big bowl of *gnocchetti con finferli*. Naturally, finferli became my favourite mushrooms. The elation of discovering a hoard of finferli is akin to coming down the stairs on Christmas morning and finding a present under the tree.

TO MAKE THE GNOCCHETTI, boil the potatoes in their jackets until the tip of a knife inserted into the centre slides through easily. Once cooked, remove the fluffy potatoes from their skins. Place the potatoes in a bowl and mash. Add the flour and mix well. Incorporate the beaten egg yolk and the wine and knead lightly.

SERVES 6

4 tablespoons extra virgin olive oil

20g sun-dried tomatoes, finely sliced

2 garlic cloves, finely sliced

100ml dry white wine

200g chantarelle mushrooms, left whole

½ teaspoon dried chilli flakes

150ml fresh cream

salt

50g freshly grated parmigiano

2 tablespoons chopped fresh flat-leaf parsley, to garnish

For the gnocchetti:

1kg floury potatoes, such as Maris Piper or Désirée

300g '00' flour or plain flour

1 organic or free-range egg yolk, beaten

1 tablespoon dry white wine

Turn the dough out onto a floured board. Form into long snakes about 1.5cm thick, then cut into 2cm pieces. Rub each gnocco along the back of a fork to create linear ridges. Set aside.

Heat the olive oil in a large pan over a low heat. Sauté the sun-dried tomatoes and garlic for about 1 minute, just until the garlic is fragrant but not browned. Pour in the wine and increase the heat momentarily to cook off the alcohol. Add the mushrooms and chilli flakes, cover the pan and cook for 10 minutes. Stir in the cream and cook for 1 minute more.

Cook the gnocchetti in a large saucepan of boiling salted water. They are ready as soon as they rise to the top of the saucepan, which should only take a few minutes. Drain.

Add the drained gnocchetti to the pan and season with salt to taste. Fold in the parmigiano and serve immediately, garnished with the chopped parsley.

If you won't want to make the gnocchetti, buy them from a good deli instead. Another equally delicious version would be to omit the sun-dried tomatoes and to blend the creamed mushrooms.

Calabrese swordfish *pizzaiola*

Pesce spade alla Calabrese

Nicastro, Calabria, 1980. 'Eileen, don't you just love this town?' Caterina asks as we walk the Sunday afternoon *passegiata* ritual. 'To tell you the truth, I feel very uncomfortable. Men are looking at us as if we are nude,' I reply. Nudging me affectionately in the side and tossing back her magnificent mane of jet-black hair, she laughs, '*Quelli sono sguardi d'amore.*' (Those are the stares of love.) 'Let's go home. I want to make you a really special Calabrian dish this evening of swordfish, capers and oregano. It captures the magic of Calabria.'

PREHEAT THE OVEN to 200°C.

Using an oven tray big enough to hold all the swordfish steaks, heat half of the oil in the tray over a low heat. Sauté the garlic for about 1 minute, just until it's fragrant but not browned. Remove the dish from the heat.

Lay the fish on the bottom of the tray and layer each one with a slice of buffalo mozzarella, a couple of quartered cherry tomatoes, olives, capers, oregano and basil. Finish with a generous dousing of the remaining extra virgin olive oil.

Place the tray in the hot oven and cook for about 15 minutes, until the mozzarella is nicely melted, the fish is cooked through and all of the ingredients have amalgamated.

Transfer the fish to a large serving platter, sprinkle with the parsley and serve immediately.

SERVES 6

150ml extra virgin olive oil
3 garlic cloves, crushed
6 x 150g swordfish steaks
500g buffalo mozzarella, cut into 6 slices
12 cherry tomatoes, quartered
60g black olives
20g capers, soaked and patted dry to remove excess salt
bunch of fresh oregano or 2 tablespoons dried oregano
bunch of fresh basil
2 tablespoons finely chopped fresh flat-leaf parsley

Tomatoes stuffed with saffron rice

Pomodori ripieni di riso allo zafferano

Stuffed tomatoes is one of those dishes that Italians tend to buy from the *rosticceria* (rotisserie). Food from a *rosticceria* would be considered high-end deli food in any other country, but in Italy it's just your local run-of-the-mill takeout. It's where you stop on your way home from work to pick up a roast chicken on the spit and rosemary potatoes, grilled and stuffed vegetables, pizza slices and calzone, stuffed tomatoes with roasted chips, boiled greens with olive oil and lemon juice, meat stews, *arancini* and *supplì*.

My favourite is Pizza Pazza, Via Baldovinetti, Eur, Rome, a lifesaver after an unusually hectic day in the office (or was it a usual hectic day in the office?) and four hungry children waiting to be fed. My children are all young adults now and all of them still return to Pizza Pazza for *supplì*, stuffed tomatoes and delicious pizza slices.

PREHEAT THE OVEN to 175°C. Brush the base of a baking tray with olive oil.

Cook the rice in a large saucepan of boiling salted water until al dente or according to the packet instructions and drain well.

Cut the caps off the tomatoes and set them aside to use later. Scoop the pulp from the tomatoes and place it in a bowl. Blend the pulp with a hand blender.

MAKES 12

320g Arborio, Carnaroli or Vialone Nano rice

12 ripe beef tomatoes

4 tablespoons extra virgin olive oil

1 garlic clove, peeled and left whole

1 sachet of saffron

5 fresh basil leaves

1 tablespoon dried oregano or small bunch of fresh oregano, chopped

pinch of salt

50g freshly grated Pecorino

1 ball of smoked mozzarella, cut into cubes (optional)

Heat the olive oil in a medium saucepan over a low heat. Sauté the garlic for about 1 minute, just until it's fragrant but not browned. Remove the garlic with a slotted spoon. Add the blended pulp to the pan along with the saffron, basil, oregano and a generous pinch of salt. Cover and cook for 10 minutes. Stir the drained rice into the sauce along with the grated Pecorino cheese.

Fill each tomato halfway with rice. Nestle a piece of smoked mozzarella into the rice, if using, and continue to fill with rice to the top of the tomato. Replace the caps on top of the tomatoes.

Sit the tomatoes close together in the oiled tray and bake for 1 hour, until the tomatoes have crinkled. Serve one stuffed tomato per person.

Stuffed tomatoes are traditionally served with fat oven chips that are cooked in the same tin as the tomatoes.

Romanesco broccoli and anchovies

Broccoli romaneschi ripassati con alici

My sister Sheila lives in Rome, and this is the dish she makes best. I always call her before I arrive and ask her to prepare her Romanesco broccoli, as I can eat several bowls of it. She will have set an alluring table with a multitude of candles, colourful glasses and shiny crockery, boards of cheese and salumi and the vivid green broccoli taking centre stage. It's simple, beautiful, homely and welcoming: 'Ah, here you are at last.'

COOK THE BROCCOLI in plenty of boiling salted water for 5 minutes, until al dente. Drain and keep back a cup of the cooking water.

Heat the oil in a large pan (a wok is best) over a low heat. Sauté the garlic and anchovies for about 1 minute, just until the garlic is fragrant but not browned. Using a wooden spoon, lightly mash the anchovies to dissolve them in the oil.

Add the drained broccoli to the pan along with the reserved cup of water. Cover the pan and cook for 5 more minutes, then transfer to a serving dish and serve immediately.

SERVES 4 (OR ONE EILEEN!)

1kg broccoli florets (use Romanesco if you can find it)

4 tablespoons extra virgin olive oil

4 garlic cloves, peeled and left whole

4 anchovies

If you can't find Romanesco broccoli, regular broccoli works just as well.

· 156 ·

Marsala plums with whipped cream

Prugne al marsala con panna

My brother Rory lives next door to me and is always in and out of my house, checking on what I am cooking. We exchange dishes and cooking tips on an almost daily basis. He cooks amazing Asian food and naturally I cook mostly Italian. There are 15 years between us and I like to think he is an excellent cook because of my influence, having cultivated his curiosity about food from a young age, but probably not with the love and diplomacy he deserved.

When I left for Italy he was only two years old and on my visits home I would constantly barrage him and my mother about his eating habits, i.e. he didn't eat like Italian children. My poor mother had the patience of a saint as I would insist on her buying him a little fish or meat, steaming it along with loads of vegetables and blending it all together with a glug of extra virgin olive oil (which I religiously brought home with me). 'You have him eating rabbit food,' she would say, 'and what's wrong with butter? You're putting that stuff for earaches on his dinner!' At that time in Ireland, you could only get olive oil in a chemist and people used it for earaches.

Continued overleaf

SERVES 6

1kg plums, halved and stones removed
200g caster sugar
250ml good Marsala dessert wine
250ml fresh cream
fresh mint sprigs, to decorate

Roll on the years and we are great pals, my brother and I. His favourite dessert is Marsala plums with whipped cream. We have tried plums with mascarpone, vanilla and pistachio ice cream, but he vehemently swears that plums and cream are the supreme combination.

Simmer the plums, sugar and Marsala in a saucepan on a medium heat for 20 minutes, until the plums are soft and the sauce is nice and syrupy.

Meanwhile, whip the cream in a mixing bowl just until soft peaks form.

Remove the plums with a slotted spoon and divide between six dessert glasses. Spoon over the juices from the pan and serve with a good dollop of whipped cream and a sprig of fresh mint to decorate.

Grate dark chocolate shavings or sprinkle toasted almond flakes on top, but don't tell Rory!

LABOUR DAY PICNIC

Primo Maggio

PRESENT
Family and friends

....

ANTIPASTO
Pecorino and broad bean salad

PASTA
Farfalle pasta salad with cherry tomatoes, tuna, pine nuts and mandarins
Rice salad with tuna and pickles

MAINS
Tropea red onion, pancetta and potato frittata

SIDES
Cannellini bean, celery, sun-dried tomato and avocado salad

DESSERT
Lemon *ciambella* with pistachio glaze

BELLA CIAO*, *bella ciao, bella ciao ciao ciao* is a

catchy anthem that I have taught to most of my non-Italian friends. The song is about a dying freedom fighter who wants to be buried on the side of a mountain under the shade of a beautiful flower. *Bella ciao* (beautiful goodbye) was the anthem of the Italian anti-fascist movement during and after the Second World War. Putting aside the political connotations, it's an irresistible tune that everyone loves.

The May 1st open-air late-evening concert at the imposing Basilica of San Giovanni in Rome is a tradition and is broadcast live to every corner of Italy. Thousands gather each year under the imposing cathedral, once the seat of popes, and the ancient Egyptian Lateran Obelisk that was ripped from the temple in Karnak. It draws a multigenerational sea of individuals: young people who come to hear their favourite groups play live and older people who come to reminisce about the concerts of years past. The *bella ciao* anthem weaves in and out intermittently between the rock and the jazz and everyone joins in.

After each and every concert, Stefano never fails to be amazed at the massive amount of objects left lying around. 'Surely we didn't discard beer and wine bottles and empty cigarette packets, abandon scarves, jackets and hats, and generally disrespect the square of the gods,' he laments. '*Ciao bello*,' I respond in true Roman style, eyes raised to heaven with a disrespectful wave of my hand.

On Labour Day, yet another prominent Italian *festa*, families head for the nearest woodland and spend the day collecting *pinoli* (pine nuts), crushing them open with heavy stones, and wild mushrooms and munching on heaps of homemade food.

Pecorino and broad bean salad

Insalatina di fave e pecorino

Pecorino and broad beans go hand in hand with the *Primo Maggio* (Labour Day) picnic.

BOIL THE SHELLED BROAD BEANS in a pot of salted water for a couple of minutes. Drain and place in a bowl of cold water. Squeeze the beans from their skins and discard the skins.

Toss the broad beans, lettuce and cheese with a drizzle of olive oil and freshly squeezed lemon juice. Enjoy with crusty bread or breadsticks.

SERVES 4–6

500g new season shelled broad beans
300g lamb's lettuce or rocket
250g mature Pecorino Romano or
    similar salty cheese shavings
extra virgin olive oil
juice of 1 lemon
crusty bread or breadsticks, to serve

Farfalle pasta salad with cherry tomatoes, tuna, pine nuts and mandarins

Farfalle con pomodorini, tonno, pinoli e mandarino

Farfalle is perfect for cold pasta salads, as this pasta tends to keep its bite and children love the butterfly shape.

COOK THE PASTA in a large saucepan of boiling salted water until al dente or according to the packet instructions. Drain well and place in a large serving dish.

Toast the pine nuts on a hot, dry pan for 30 seconds, taking care not to let them burn.

Mix the pasta together with the rest of the ingredients (except the basil) while the pasta is still hot. Spread out on a tray and leave to cool.

Once cool, fold through the chopped basil leaves and pack for the picnic.

SERVES 6

500g farfalle pasta
25g pine nuts
200g cherry tomatoes, halved
200g yellowfin tuna preserved in oil
6 mandarins, peeled and segmented
150ml extra virgin olive oil
a couple fresh basil leaves, chopped

It's important to mix the ingredients with the pasta while it's still warm. Warm pasta will absorb the flavours of the other ingredients; cold pasta will not.

Rice salad with tuna and pickles

Insalata di riso

Insalata di riso is a good dish to keep in the fridge when members of your household are coming home at different times of the day, such as teenagers or young adults returning in the early hours after a night on the town. Everyone can help themselves.

COOK THE RICE in a large saucepan of boiling salted water according to the packet instructions. Drain well and place in a large bowl.

Place the eggs in a saucepan and cover well with cold water. Bring to the boil, then cover the pan and remove it from the heat. Leave to stand for 12 minutes. Remove the eggs from the water with a slotted spoon and run under cold water to cool them quickly. Once cooled, peel and slice the eggs.

Mix the hot rice with the sliced eggs, pickles, tuna, ham, mortadella (if using) and 100ml of the olive oil. Spread out on a tray and leave to cool.

Stir in the cheese, parsley and the remaining 100ml olive oil and season to taste with salt and pepper, then pack for the picnic.

SERVES 8

360g long grain rice

4 free-range or organic eggs

500g mixed pickles, such as gherkins, carrots and onions, chopped

250g yellowfin tuna preserved in oil

200g thick-sliced good-quality ham, chopped into small cubes

100g thick-sliced mortadella, chopped into small cubes (optional)

200ml extra virgin olive oil

200g parmigiano, Pecorino or a mature Cheddar, cut into small cubes

2 tablespoons finely chopped fresh flat-leaf parsley

salt and freshly ground black pepper

Tropea red onion, pancetta and potato frittata

Frittata di cipolle di tropea, pancetta e patate

Tropea onions hail from the Nicotera area of Calabria. They are beautiful, sweet and intensely red. I cannot convey how different these onions actually are and to what extent they can enhance a dish. When you use them, a simple frittata becomes gourmet food.

HEAT 2 TABLESPOONS of olive oil in a 28cm non-stick pan over a medium heat. Sauté the onion for 5 minutes and remove from the pan. Add a little more oil to the pan and fry the boiled potato slices and the pancetta until the pancetta is cooked through and crispy. Remove from the heat and allow to cool a little.

Beat the eggs in a medium-sized bowl, then mix in the onion, potato and pancetta and some salt and pepper.

Wipe out the pan and coat the bottom with 2 tablespoons of olive oil. Set over a medium heat, then pour in the egg mixture. Shake the pan lightly to spread the eggs evenly.

When the egg starts to set, gently pull the frittata from the edges of the pan. Place a large dinner plate over the pan and turn it over so that the frittata is now sitting on the plate. Slide the frittata back into the pan to cook the other side for about 2 minutes.

Cut into triangles, allow to cool and pack for the picnic.

SERVES 6–8

extra virgin olive oil

1 medium Tropea red onion, thinly sliced (or a regular red or white onion)

1 boiled potato, sliced

50g finely sliced pancetta, cut into strips

8 free-range or organic eggs, beaten

salt and freshly ground black pepper

Cold frittata is very nice between two thick slices of focaccia as a lunchtime sandwich.

Cannellini bean, celery, sun-dried tomato and avocado salad

Insalata di fagioli cannellini, sedano, mela e avocado

When you think of salads, you don't necessarily have to incorporate leaves. Beans absorb dressings such as olive oil and vinegar nicely and provide a good base on which to build a salad. My vegetarian daughter, Federica, loves such salads.

Italian cuisine is ideal for vegetarians. There is no need to invent specific vegetarian dishes, as there are already so many suitable dishes on the Italian menu. A vegetarian can feel comfortable in most Italian restaurants. Italians tend to eat a little meat, fish, cheese, salumi and an abundance of vegetables and fruits. All my Italian friends, family and acquaintances would be quite happy with an Italian vegetarian diet – they wouldn't miss the meat, but they cannot do without fresh fruit and vegetables.

PLACE ALL THE SALAD INGREDIENTS together in a large serving bowl.

Put all the dressing ingredients in a screw-top jar and shake to combine. Pour over the salad and mix well.

SERVES 4

250g tinned cannellini beans, drained and rinsed
25g soft sun-dried tomatoes, shredded
2 avocados, peeled and chopped
2 celery sticks, diced

For the dressing:
100ml extra virgin olive oil
juice of ½ lemon
1 teaspoon wholegrain honey mustard
salt and freshly ground black pepper

Play around with ingredients, such as sun-dried tomatoes, mango and crushed walnuts, or use borlotti beans and chickpeas.

Lemon *ciambella* with pistachio glaze

Ciambellone

Fancy, dainty cakes called *pastarelle* are for Sundays and are traditionally bought in the *pasticceria* (pastry shop), where they are neatly piled onto gold cardboard trays, wrapped in lovely waxed paper and tied up with beautiful ribbons. When you are invited to Sunday lunch, you must take along a beautifully packaged tray of dainty *mignon* cakes. There will be much fanfare around the opening of your packet and you will discover that everyone has a different favourite.

It can be difficult, therefore, to understand the Italian love of *ciambellone* given its simplicity. *Ciambellone* is an everyday homemade cake eaten for breakfast spread with jam or as a *merenda* (mid-morning or afternoon snack) with tea and coffee, and when stale it is dunked in wine after dinner. *Genuina*, which means genuine and homemade, is the key adjective that is usually applied to the *ciambellone*, so it's a given that it has to be good. My pistachio glaze adds a baroque embellishment to the cake.

When my young son Ghinlon attended junior school, one of the class mothers was expected to make the *merenda* each Friday. It was usually a *ciambellone* or a *crostata* (jam tart). Naturally, Ghinlon always told me just before retiring on the Thursday evening that it was my turn. What else could I do at that stage other than whip up a few batches of fairy cakes? On a previous occasion I had tried to pass off a bought *crostata* from the local Jewish bakery as a home bake, but my dear friend and

SERVES 12

80ml milk
1 vanilla pod
200g butter, softened
200g granulated sugar
4 free-range or organic eggs
300g self-raising flour
200g cornflour
2 teaspoons baking powder
zest of 1 lemon
pinch of salt

For the pistachio glaze:
50g caster sugar
50g shelled pistachios, plus extra
    crushed pistachios to decorate
zest and juice of 1 lemon

neighbour, Nadia, was sent by the parents' committee to explain to me that the *merenda* must be *genuina*. This was a competitive business. The parents waited at the school gate every Friday, ready to interrogate their *bambini* on the *bontà* – the goodness of the *merenda*.

Apparently the fairy cakes went down a treat, so I was surprised to receive a call over the weekend from one of the mothers, Camilla. Camilla was a downright snob who spoke with the *erre moscia* (soft *r*) and an unbearable high-pitched, child-like voice. '*Signora*,' she started (remember her soft *r*!), 'I just wanted to let you know that you mustn't use cake formulas for the children's *merendas*. I wonder if those cakes you made were Betty Crocker.'

'No,' I replied. 'They were Betty Carlyon.'

In a higher than usual pitch, she squeaked, '*Ma signora, non si può!*' (Signora, you cannot!) At which point I interrupted her, with a touch of haughtiness: 'Betty Carlyon was my grandmother's sister, a renowned baker, and those cakes are her recipe.' She took a seemingly exaggeratedly long breath and said, '*Grazie a Dio.*' (Thank God.) But I didn't stop there. 'Actually, the eggs are from my *portiera's* (concierge's) brother's farm, along with some good Irish butter and a little flour.'

Continued overleaf

The news spread from mother to mother. Everyone not only wanted the recipe, but they wanted my *portiera's* brother's farm-fresh eggs too. What could I do but buy them at the market and pass them off? After a couple of weeks it was costing me a fortune and I was burdened with guilt. It had to end. I decided that the *portiera's* brother died, but he didn't die simply of a heart attack. No, he was crushed by a wild boar, which definitively meant no more eggs.

All was well until one day I met Nadia outside of my doorway and my *portiera*, Laura, happened to pass by. 'Sorry for your loss, *signora*,' Nadia said. 'Weren't those eggs marvellous?' The *portiera* thought she had lost the plot. '*Ma quella è pazza* (that one is mad),' she whispered to me and scurried into the cool shadows of the hallway.

PREHEAT THE OVEN to 180°C. Grease a 24cm savarin cake tin or a fluted savarin tin.

Put the milk in a small saucepan. Cut the vanilla pod lengthways and scrape the seeds into the milk. Warm the milk and set aside.

Cream together the butter and sugar until pale and fluffy. Add the eggs one by one and mix until well incorporated. Fold in the flour, cornflour, baking powder, lemon zest and a pinch of salt. Moisten with the warm milk and mix again until just combined.

Pour the batter into the greased tin. Bake in the oven for 40 minutes, until a skewer comes out clean. Leave to rest in the tin for 10 minutes before turning out the cake onto a wire rack to cool.

To make the pistachio glaze, gently heat all of the ingredients in a small pot. Pour over the cake for a stunning result and decorate with whole or crushed pistachios, or both.

A sugar icing is suitable for children or guests who are allergic to nuts. Place 200g icing sugar in a bowl and gradually add 2 tablespoons of warm water. Stir continuously until you have a nice, soft, thick icing to drizzle over the top of the ciambellone.

RELIGIOUS FESTIVITIES

Festivà Religiose

PRESENT

Family, friends and relatives

....

ANTIPASTO

Sauté of clams with toast

Bresaola, robiola and honey rolls

PASTA

Risotto with white asparagus, scallops and saffron

Trofie with pesto and prawns

MAINS

Cod with prawn cream sauce

Roast stuffed chicken

SIDES

Olive oil and rosemary chips

DESSERT

Pizza with peaches and mistrà

GIVEN that the Catholic Church has its headquarters in Rome, Italy has

traditionally been a Catholic country operating within a secular state. The Catholic Church continuously interferes in state matters, but the Italian constitution provides for the practice and respect of all religions. Italian regional cuisine is a fusion of many cultures and religions, which is what makes it unique and wonderful. Whether the occasion is a baptism, bat/bar mitzvah or post-Ramadan feast, these are all opportunities for celebration. *Che la festa cominci* – let the party begin.

Sauté of clams with toast

Zuppa di vongole con pane tostato

This is called a *zuppa*, or soup, but it isn't a soup as we know it. The combination of fresh clams, white wine and garlic makes the most enjoyable sauce. Expect shouts for more bread to mop up the savoury juices.

I suggest you undertake the following in two batches.

RINSE THE CLAMS in cold water. Tap any open clams on the side of a plate or the counter, and if they don't close, discard them.

Heat the oil in a large saucepan or wok over a low heat. Sauté the garlic for about 1 minute, just until it's fragrant but not browned. Add the chilli flakes and tomatoes and cook for 2 minutes. Add the clams and lemon zest and pour in the wine. Increase the heat momentarily to cook off the alcohol.

Cover the pot and cook for a couple of minutes more, until all of the clams have opened.

Preheat the oven grill and toast the bread on one side. Drizzle with extra virgin olive oil and a little salt and pepper.

Serve a good helping of clams with some of the juices and two slices of toast placed at the side of each dish. Garnish with a little finely chopped fresh parsley. Don't forget to put a big plate in the centre of the table for the empty clam shells.

SERVES 6–8

2kg clams, scrubbed
8 tablespoons extra virgin olive oil
8 garlic cloves, peeled and left whole
2 level teaspoons dried chilli flakes
16 cherry tomatoes, quartered
zest of 2 lemons
300ml dry white wine
12 thick slices of country bread
salt and freshly ground black pepper
2 tablespoons finely chopped fresh
    flat-leaf parsley

Bread for soaking up the scrumptious sauce is essential. It's called fare la scarpetta— *'to make a small shoe'. It involves taking a piece of bread and moulding it into a small shoe-like recipient for sauce. Soaking up sauce in this way is considered to be a compliment to your host. Of course, we are talking about informal dinners – I don't suggest you ask for bread* per fare la scarpetta *when you are dining at a Michelin-starred restaurant.*

Bresaola, robiola and honey rolls

Involtini di bresaola, robiola e miele

Bresaola rolls are quick and easy to make and never fail to impress.

PLACE A THICK STRIP OF CHEESE along the middle of a slice of bresaola and drizzle with honey. Fold the bresaola to form little rolls. Serve on a bed of rocket dressed with lemon juice.

MAKES 24 ROLLS

500g robiola cheese (or you can use ricotta, mascarpone or soft goat's cheese)

24 wafer-thin slices of bresaolo

150ml runny honey

150g rocket

juice of ½ lemon

Bresaola has a very high iron content and is perfect if you are feeling under the weather.

Risotto with white asparagus, scallops and saffron

Risotto con asparagi bianchi, capesante e zafferano

There is something eerily beautiful, almost holy, about white asparagus. Risotto with white asparagus, Pinot Grigio and a shot of grappa is a celebration of the Veneto cuisine.

BEND THE ASPARAGUS until it naturally snaps and discard the woody ends. Cook the asparagus in 1 litre of boiling salted water for 5 minutes and remove with a slotted spoon. Cut into 2cm pieces and set aside.

Add the shallot, carrot, celery stick and a generous seasoning of salt and pepper to the water you cooked the asparagus in to make a broth for the risotto. Simmer on a low heat for 30 minutes in a covered saucepan. Remove the vegetables with a slotted spoon and keep the broth hot.

Heat the olive oil in a large, wide, heavy-based saucepan over a low heat. Sauté the shallots for 5 minutes, until they are soft and translucent. Add the rice and cook for 1 minute. Add half of the asparagus and half of the sliced scallops and stir. Pour in the grappa, if using, and cook for 1 minute, then pour in the wine. Increase the heat momentarily to cook off the alcohol.

Dissolve the saffron in a ladle of broth and add to the rice. Add the hot broth one ladleful at a time. Stir constantly until all the broth has been absorbed before adding the next ladle. Keep adding the broth bit by bit and stirring until all the broth has been absorbed, which should take about 20 minutes.

When the rice is cooked (it should still have a bite to it), stir in the rest of the asparagus and scallops. Cook for another 5 minutes, then stir in the knob of butter. Serve immediately.

SERVES 6

1kg white asparagus or 600g green asparagus
1 litre cold water
4 tablespoons extra virgin olive oil
2 shallots, finely sliced
360g Carnaroli or Arborio rice
500g scallops, finely sliced (you can use the corals as well)
1 shot of grappa (optional)
150ml Pinot Grigio or white wine of your choice
1 x 2g sachet of saffron powder or saffron threads
knob of butter

For the broth:
1 shallot, peeled and left whole
1 carrot, peeled and left whole
1 celery stick
salt and freshly ground black pepper

Trofie with pesto and prawns

Trofie con pesto e gamberi

The addition of fresh prawns adds a touch of elegance and colour to this Ligurian pasta dish.

TO MAKE THE PESTO, blitz the basil, parmigiano, pine nuts, almonds and garlic in a blender with half the oil. Gradually incorporate the rest of the oil until you obtain a smooth consistency.

Cook the pasta in a large saucepan of boiling salted water until al dente or according to the packet instructions. Drain well.

Pour the pesto and 2 tablespoons of the extra virgin olive oil into a large serving bowl. Whisk together to create an emulsion.

Heat the remaining 2 tablespoons of oil in a large pan over a low heat. Sauté the prawns and garlic for about 1 minute, just until the garlic is fragrant but not browned. Remove the garlic with a slotted spoon. Add the wine and increase the heat momentarily to cook off the alcohol, then cover the pan and cook for 2 minutes.

Add the drained pasta to the serving bowl with the pesto and mix together until all the pasta is coated with the pesto. Fold in the prawns and serve immediately.

SERVES 6–8

500g trofie or casarecce pasta
4 tablespoons extra virgin olive oil
500g prawns, washed and shelled
1 garlic clove, peeled and left whole
100ml white wine

For the pesto:
100g fresh basil leaves
100g freshly grated parmigiano
50g pine nuts
30 peeled almonds
2 garlic cloves, crushed
150ml extra virgin olive oil

Always use cold pesto to fold into the dish.

Cod with prawn cream sauce

Merluzzo con crema di scampi

A noble sauce for our dear cod.

TO MAKE THE SAUCE, remove the heads and tails from the prawns. Place the heads and tails in a saucepan along with the onion, carrot, celery stick and a generous seasoning of salt. Pour over the water and simmer for 30 minutes. Strain the broth and discard the rest.

Meanwhile, heat the olive oil and a knob of butter in a large pan over a low heat. Sauté the prawns and shallots for 1 minute. Pour in the brandy and raise the heat momentarily to cook off the alcohol. Add the broth and cook for a couple more minutes. Blitz with a hand blender and stir in the cream.

Gently poach the cod fillets in a pan of simmering water for 5 minutes. Place a fillet of fish in each of six pasta bowls, pour over the sauce and garnish with chopped parsley.

SERVES 6

6 x 150–200g cod fillets
bunch of fresh flat-leaf parsley,
    roughly chopped

For the prawn cream sauce:
600g Dublin Bay prawns
1 medium onion, peeled and left
    whole
1 carrot, peeled and left whole
1 celery stick
salt
1 litre water
4 tablespoons extra virgin olive oil
knob of butter
1 shallot, finely sliced
100ml brandy
500ml fresh cream

The prawn cream sauce is wonderful with tonnarelli pasta or as a risotto con crema di scampi.

Roast stuffed chicken

Pollo ripieno

My brother-in-law settled into his first posting as a doctor in a quirky *borgo* (hamlet) in the Lazio countryside. He did so with enthusiasm but also trepidation, knowing that valuable experience might require patience and persistence. Shortly after he moved in I took my daughter for a check-up, crossing the enclosed cobblestone piazza to his Studio Medico. We took our place on a bench beside a number of villagers – toothless men and rounded women. Each held a precious gift and gazed at their neighbours' offerings with envy: cheese and salami wrapped in butcher paper and tied with twine, a caged rabbit, a *pollo ruspante* (free-range chicken) resting in a vegetable crate, baskets of fruit and vegetables, cakes and biscotti wrapped in tin foil, and bottles of wine and olive oil. One blushing lady held a pot enveloped in a crisp dishcloth on her wide lap. Curiosity got the better of me and I asked what was in it. She whipped off the cloth and opened the pot, releasing a fantastic aroma. '*Spezzatino, spezzatino di manzo per il medico*,' she said (stew, beef stew for the doctor). She stood up and showed off her stew to all present, returned the lid, retied the cloth and took her seat with a conceited smile. 'We have enough cakes, biscotti and bread to open a pastry shop and enough chickens, salami and cheese to run a restaurant,' Stefano's sister would say, 'and while we will never go hungry, it would be nice to have a little money for a rainy day.'

Continued overleaf

SERVES 12

4 Italian salsiccia sausages
knob of butter
2 shallots, finely diced
500g fresh breadcrumbs
2 tablespoons fresh thyme leaves
salt and freshly ground black
    pepper
2 medium free-range or organic
    chickens, each cut into 6 pieces
1 lemon
a few sprigs of fresh rosemary

Leabharlanna Poibli Chathair Baile Átha Cliath
Dublin City Public Libraries

PREHEAT THE OVEN to 250°C.

To make the stuffing, squeeze the sausagemeat out of its skin.
Melt the butter in a large saucepan over a low heat. When it's
foaming, gently fry the shallots for 2 or 3 minutes, until they are
soft and translucent. Add the sausagemeat and cook for 2
minutes. Stir in the breadcrumbs, thyme and some salt and
pepper. Remove from the heat.

Place a good knob of stuffing under the skin of each chicken
piece. Cut the lemon in half and rub the skin of the chicken with
lemon juice.

Place the chicken pieces in an ungreased oven dish, skin side
down. Lay the rosemary sprigs on top. Roast for 10 minutes, then
turn the chicken over and cook for 35 minutes more, until the
chicken is cooked through and the skin is crisp and golden brown.

*You might like to use a
variety of herbs, such as
tarragon or coriander.*

Olive oil and rosemary chips

Patatine al forno all'olio d'oliva

There is nothing as nice as fat oven chips cooked in olive oil – golden brown on the outside, soft and bright white on the inside and scented with rosemary.

PREHEAT THE OVEN to 250℃.

Cut the potatoes lengthways into 1cm slices, then cut each slice into a 2cm chip. Place the chips in a wide oven dish.

Pour over the olive oil and salt. Mix well, incorporating the rosemary. Bake for 20–25 minutes, until golden brown.

SERVES 6

500g medium Maris Piper or
    Rooster potatoes, peeled
200ml extra virgin olive oil
1 tablespoon coarse sea salt
sprig of fresh rosemary

Pizza with peaches and mistrà

Pizza con pesche al forno e mistrà

Our local bar and *pizzeria* in the Marche is where we have our cappuccino in the morning, our after-lunch espresso, our evening *aperitivo* and our late-night after-dinner *digestivo*. It's a *ritrovo*: a place where locals get together and chat, gossip, read the local newspapers, play cards and generally pass the time of day. Rickety old chairs are moved from one side of the street to the other chasing the shade. On Sundays the villagers chat, gossip, read the local newspapers and play cards just like every other day, but being Sunday, one dares not step outside the door casually dressed. When we first moved in we raised the odd eyebrow or two with our children who didn't attend mass, wore flip-flops on Sundays and ate between meals. Tersilia, the bar owner, concerned that our children were eating too much of her wonderful pizza, prepared huge casserole dishes of Swiss chard to make sure they got their greens. Tersilia also managed to hook the adults on pizza with peaches and mistrà, a lovely dessert for sharing. Mistrà, an aniseed-based liquor, can be known to evoke the unsuspected.

To MAKE THE PIZZA DOUGH, dissolve the yeast and sugar in the warm water in a small bowl and let it stand for 10 minutes, until the yeast is frothy.

Continued overleaf

MAKES 2 LARGE PIZZAS

6 ripe peaches or a jar of peaches in syrup, sliced
250ml mistrà, Pernod or pastis
knob of butter, for greasing
250g mascarpone (optional)
icing sugar, for dusting

For the pizza dough:
1 x 7g sachet fast action dried yeast
1 teaspoon caster sugar
250ml warm water
500g plain flour
2 tablespoons extra virgin olive oil
pinch of salt

Pour the flour onto a wooden board and form and mound. Make a well in the middle of the mound and pour the activated yeast mixture, oil and salt into the well. Using your fingers, start to mix the flour with the liquid. Start around the edges of the well and gradually incorporate all of the flour. Knead the dough for a good 10 minutes, until it's smooth and elastic. Alternatively, you could use a food mixer fitted with a dough hook.

Brush two large bowls for proving the dough with olive oil. Divide the dough in half and knead again to form two smooth balls. Place each ball in an oiled bowl and cover with a clean, damp cloth. Leave to rise in a warm place for about 2 hours, until the dough has doubled in size.

While the dough is proving, place the peaches in a bowl and pour over the mistrà. Refrigerate for 2 hours.

Preheat the oven to 200°C. Grease two large baking trays with butter.

Turn the dough out onto a floured surface. Knock it back and knead for a couple of minutes. Roll it out into two large rectangles. Using your hands, stretch out the dough to cover each tray. Bake in the hot oven for 20 minutes.

While the pizzas are baking, char the peaches on a hot griddle pan for 1 minute on each side. Remove the pizzas from the oven and arrange the charred peaches on top. Return to the oven for just a minute, then remove. Dot with mascarpone, if using, and dust with icing sugar. Leave to rest for a couple of minutes before cutting into squares or rectangles. This is best served hot, as it doesn't reheat well.

Allow a decent time span between the main course and dessert, then out of the blue, say, 'Anyone for pizza with peaches and mistrà for dessert?' Your guests will be stunned – 'pizza for dessert?' – and it will become your party piece.

BIRTHDAY AND NAMES DAY DINNER

Compleanno e Onomastico

PRESENT

Family, friends and close relatives

....

ANTIPASTO

Caponata vegetable antipasto

RISOTTO

Risotto with mushrooms and duck perfumed with thyme

MAINS

Meatballs with apricot and basil compote

SIDES

Warm asparagus salad

DESSERT

Tiramisù with vin santo

BIRTHDAYS are a big event in Italy and I make

sure I'm there for mine every year. Celebrations go on for at least a week and presents are plentiful. The family dinner is something of a culinary competition, with everyone bringing a dish that will be discussed in minute detail, hailed at the table and critiqued in whispers in the kitchen. This all-important dinner must occur on the actual day of the birthday. Italians will not celebrate prior to the exact date as it might bring bad luck – just what kind of bad luck, I have never understood. Then there is a fun dinner in a restaurant with friends, lunch with colleagues and former colleagues and the odd dinner with those who couldn't make any of the other events. Birthdays are an opportunity to celebrate and get together, no matter what age you are.

Gifts tend to be thoughtful and beautifully wrapped. *La bella figura*, making a good impression, is important and attractive gift-wrapping is part of it. But it goes beyond that. Wrapping something nicely is respectful and caring, and unwrapping a present releases that inner child in all of us.

My own mother, who was something of a shopaholic (a trait her daughters may have inherited), couldn't resist special offers, which she stored in a great big cabinet in her bedroom. Whenever a gift was required, she rummaged through the boxes, bags and bric-a-brac and pulled out the most bizarre things. Her gifts were rarely appropriate. Each year she gives Stefano a packet of multicoloured short socks, oblivious to the rigorous dress code of Italian men, who all wear knee-high monotone *filo di scozia* (fine cotton socks). Before your imagination runs wild, there is actually some logic behind the knee-high socks. You will note that when Italian men sit down, you never see a stark white hairy band between the sock and the trousers. So ladies and gents, do your menfolk a favour and buy them Italian socks.

Caponata vegetable antipasto

Caponata, un antipasto di verdura ideale

Preserving vegetables in oil, salt or vinegar or simply by drying them is a transformative process. A new product is born that can be enjoyed in a number of ways. Consider the simple tomato, which is wonderful eaten raw and fresh, but can also be enjoyed sun-dried or preserved in olive oil and then used in different ways. Preserving food not only provides nourishment throughout the year, it creates variation in the diet and enriches a nation's culinary experience. But the jars of preserved vegetables on supermarket shelves can be somewhat of a letdown. Olive oil is expensive, so cheaper and often quite nasty oils are used. Instead, why not make a fresh and tasty *caponata*? It's a dish that you can offer to your guests either as a starter or to accompany your main fish or meat dishes and it will be highly appreciated by your vegetarian friends. Your family will never grow weary of *caponata* and you will still be making it in twenty years' time.

CUT THE AUBERGINE into 2cm cubes. Deseed the peppers and cut into strips 1cm wide. Cut a thin slice off each end of the courgettes and discard, then cut the courgette into thin slices.

Toast the pine nuts on a hot, dry pan for 2 minutes, taking care not to let them burn. Remove from the heat and set aside.

SERVES 6

2 medium aubergines
2 medium peppers
2 medium courgettes
2 tablespoons pine nuts
extra virgin olive oil
200ml white wine vinegar
4 shallots, finely diced
4 tinned anchovies (optional)
1 celery stick, diced
50g stoned black olives
20g capers, rinsed
4 fresh basil leaves (don't use dried)
200ml tomato passata
2 tablespoons granulated sugar
100ml warm water
pinch of salt

Heat a splash of extra virgin olive oil in a large pan over a medium heat. Fry the aubergines for a couple of minutes, then pour in the vinegar. Increase the heat momentarily, then reduce the heat to low. Cover the pan and cook the aubergines for 10 minutes.

Meanwhile, heat another splash of olive oil in a separate saucepan and sweat the shallots for 5 minutes over a low heat. Add the anchovies to the same saucepan, if using. Mash them with a wooden spoon to blend them into the oil.

Add the peppers, cover and cook for 10 minutes. Add the courgettes and celery, cover and cook for another 5 minutes. Now add the fried aubergines, olives, rinsed capers, fresh basil leaves, tomato passata and sugar and stir.

Pour in the warm water and a good pinch of salt. Cover and cook for 10 minutes more over a low heat, then sprinkle with toasted pine nuts.

Delicious served warm or cold with toasted ciabatta or breadsticks.

Risotto with mushrooms and duck perfumed with thyme

Risotto ai funghi con petto d'anatra al profumo di timo

Emerging from the Giorgione museum in Castelfranco Veneto and feeling both elated and famished, we stopped an elderly well-dressed gentleman to ask where would be the best place to have a good risotto. *Chiedi a uno del posto* (ask a local) is an Italian way. With a tilt of his head, he indicated that we should follow him as he led us through a maze of small streets. He never said a word, but held up his walking stick, conveying that we should stay behind him. He pushed open a tiny door and we proceeded through a dimly lit hallway and up three flights of stairs. Still not saying a word, he took his key from his waistcoat pocket and opened the door with one deft turn. '*Abbiamo compagnia*,' he called – we have company. In response, a lovely round woman in a navy wraparound apron appeared. She hugged us like she was expecting us, took our coats and set places for us at the table in her tiny kitchen.

The risotto was utter heaven. Although we tried in vain to speak Italian with our hosts and express our gratitude, they seemed to think that *stranieri* (foreigners) don't speak Italian. The *signora* shouted, presuming that foreigners will obviously understand a loud tone much more easily, and all the while her husband sat quietly nodding his head in affirmation of whatever the *signora* said. At the end of the meal, we fondly hugged again and promised to drop by some time soon. Life takes us on these unexpected journeys, which leave a warm and unforgettable imprint on our souls.

To make a broth for the risotto, fill a saucepan with 1 litre of cold water. Add in the vegetables and a generous seasoning of salt and pepper. Bring to the boil, then reduce the heat to low

SERVES 6

8 tablespoons extra virgin olive oil
2 garlic cloves, peeled and left whole
2 skinless duck breasts, diced into
    1cm pieces
2 sprigs of fresh thyme
200ml dry white wine
200g button mushrooms, sliced
2 shallots, finely sliced
360g Carnaroli or Arborio rice
1 teaspoon salt
50g freshly grated parmigiano
50g butter

For the broth:
1 litre cold water
1 shallot, peeled and left whole
1 carrot, peeled and left whole
1 celery stick
salt and freshly ground black pepper

and simmer for 30 minutes, covered. Remove the vegetables with a slotted spoon and discard them. Keep the broth hot.

Heat 2 tablespoons of the olive oil in a large pan over a low heat. Sauté one of the garlic cloves for about 1 minute, just until it's fragrant but not browned. Remove with a slotted spoon and discard. Increase the heat to medium, then add the duck and one sprig of thyme and brown the duck in the oil. Pour in half of the wine and increase the heat momentarily to cook off the alcohol. Cover and cook for 15 minutes, until the duck is tender. Stir occasionally and add a little hot water if it looks too dry. Discard the thyme.

In a separate saucepan, heat 2 tablespoons of olive oil over a low heat. Sauté the remaining garlic clove for about 1 minute, just until it's fragrant but not browned. Remove with a slotted spoon and discard. Add the mushrooms and cook for 5 minutes, until they are lightly browned.

Heat the remaining 4 tablespoons of olive oil in a large, wide, heavy-based saucepan over a low heat. Sauté the shallots and the remaining sprig of thyme for 5 minutes, until the shallots become soft and translucent. Add the rice and cook for 1 minute to let it absorb the oil. Add the duck and the teaspoon of salt, then pour in the rest of the wine. Increase the heat momentarily to cook off the alcohol. Stir in half of the mushrooms.

Add the hot broth one ladleful at a time. Stir constantly until all the broth has been absorbed before adding the next ladle. Keep adding the broth bit by bit and stirring until all the broth has been absorbed, which should take about 20 minutes.

When the rice is cooked (it should still have a bite to it), stir in the rest of the mushrooms and half of the parmigiano. Cook for another 5 minutes, then stir in the butter and the rest of the cheese. Serve immediately.

This risotto is also very good with saffron. Simply dissolve a little saffron in a ladle of broth and add to the pot halfway through the cooking. Or you could make a risotto with duck and radicchio (ideally the elongated variety from Castelfranco). Shred a head of radicchio and fry half with the shallot. Fold in the other half when the risotto is cooked.

Meatballs with apricot and basil compote

Polpette in bianco con composta di albicocche e basilico

These small morsels of meatballs are created without tomato sauce. Cooking without tomato is called *in bianco* and is considered to be *delicato* (delicate).

PUT A LITTLE FLOUR IN A SHALLOW PLATE. Combine the beef, breadcrumbs, parmigiano, shallot, egg yolk, grappa, if using, and a generous seasoning of salt and pepper in a large bowl and mix well. Use your hands to get a nice smooth finish. Pinch off a small amount and rub it between your palms to form balls the size of small plums. Roll each ball lightly in a little flour and set aside.

To make the sauce, heat the olive oil in a wide, heavy-based saucepan over a medium heat. Sauté the leeks until they soften and become translucent, then stir in the thyme, rosemary and lemon zest and a pinch of salt. Add the wine and increase the heat momentarily to cook off the alcohol.

Add the meatballs to the pan with the sauce and brown them all over. Cover and cook for 45 minutes, shaking the pot now and then to prevent them from sticking. Check regularly and add a little warm water if the sauce looks too dry.

To make the compote, place all the ingredients except the olive oil in a heavy-based saucepan and simmer for 15 minutes. Blend with a hand blender and allow to cool before stirring in the olive oil.

Serve the *polpette* with the sauce, a sprinkling of fresh thyme leaves and a spoonful of apricot and basil compote on the side for dipping.

MAKES 20 MEATBALLS

plain flour, for coating
500g minced beef
100g fresh breadcrumbs
20g freshly grated parmigiano
1 shallot, finely chopped
1 free-range or organic egg yolk, beaten
drop of grappa (optional)
salt and freshly ground black pepper

For the sauce:
4 tablespoons extra virgin olive oil
2 leeks, cleaned and thinly sliced
small sprig of fresh thyme, plus extra to garnish
small sprig of fresh rosemary
zest of 1 lemon
pinch of salt
150ml dry white wine

For the apricot and basil compote:
500g dried apricots
25g caster sugar
250ml water
zest and juice of 1 orange
6 fresh basil leaves
2 tablespoons good-quality extra virgin olive oil

Warm asparagus salad

Insalata con asparagi grigliati

When you cook for Italian guests, you must wear your thickest skin, as each dish will be mercilessly critiqued at the table. Your risotto is *buono* (good), but not as good as Gianni's mother's risotto. Your pasta is surely too al dente and Antonella's grandmother cooks her sauces for at least three hours. Grilled asparagus is not quite as good as asparagus steamed and dressed in oil and lemon. Your dinner will continue in this vein and suggestions will weave in and out of the entire evening until, alone in the kitchen, you think, 'Thank goodness I decided to buy *pasticcini* (*mignon* cakes) from the *pasticceria.*' As you delicately unwrap your beautiful package, you mention where you bought the delicacies. Silence envelops the table as you expose your chosen selection and then it all starts again. Why did you choose *diplomatica* instead of *bignè alla crema*? Don't you know that the best *pasticceria* in the area is such and such, and that you only have to go a little further for an amazing *pasticceria* specialising in *millefoglie*? By the end of the evening you will be promised umpteen recipes, which you accept graciously.

When I first went to live in Italy I was taken aback by the boldness, but at the same time I found it all fascinatingly interesting. Through these discourses, one becomes familiar with a person's family and background. Bonding is instant, and a couple of days after your dinner, the promised recipes will pour in, accompanied by small samples, such as *biscotti* and *dolci*.

SERVES 6

24 asparagus spears

2 tablespoons olive oil

150g rocket

24 firm, ripe cherry tomatoes, halved

1 small or ½ large cucumber, finely sliced

For the dressing:

6 tablespoons of your best extra virgin olive oil

2 tablespoons freshly squeezed lemon juice

1 tablespoon wholegrain honey mustard

salt and freshly ground black pepper

Rather than being offended, take it in your stride. After all, it's a way of cultivating your culinary bible. Beware, too, that if you have put on a little weight or are not looking your best, you will be greeted with, 'Oh, you have fattened,' followed by a million and one suggestions on what and what not to eat.

In our household, Stefano is sworn to silence by our daughters prior to dinners: 'Dad, don't say this' and 'Dad, don't say that'. During the meal he receives umpteen kicks under the table, to which he loudly responds, '*Adesso che ho fatto?*' – what did I do now?

BEND THE ASPARAGUS until it naturally snaps and discard the woody ends. Place the asparagus in a bowl and coat in the olive oil. Heat a griddle pan until it's smoking hot. Place the asparagus on the pan and cook for about 10 minutes, until gently charred and tender, turning them regularly.

To make the dressing, place your best olive oil, lemon juice, mustard and some salt and pepper in a screw-top jar and shake to combine the ingredients.

Place the rocket, cherry tomatoes and cucumbers on a large serving platter and toss in the salad dressing. Scatter the grilled asparagus decoratively across the top.

This salad makes a nice lunch with the addition of Asiago or Fontina cheese. And remember, if you use Italian cucumbers they need to be peeled.

Tiramisù with vin santo

Tiramisù con vin santo

I couldn't decide if I should include my tiramisù recipe in this book since it already appeared in my last one. But having asked a substantial number of Italians what their favourite Italian dessert is, the response was always the same: tiramisù. So I decided to share it once more. You will appreciate the coffee lift and the vin santo hit on a night out on the town.

SEPARATE THE EGG WHITES and yolks. In a spotlessly clean, dry bowl, whisk the whites until stiff.

In a separate large bowl, whisk together the egg yolks, mascarpone and caster sugar. Gently fold in the beaten egg whites.

Sweeten the coffee with the vin santo and granulated sugar. Pour the coffee into a shallow bowl. Holding the biscuits horizontally, dip them in the coffee one by one so that the bottom gets a brief dunk but the top stays dry. Work quickly so that the biscuits don't get soggy. Discard the leftover coffee.

Coat the bottom of a deep-sided baking dish with a layer of the mascarpone cream, followed by a layer of savoiardi. Alternate the layers until all of the ingredients have been used, finishing with a layer of the cream. Cover with cling film and refrigerate for at least 2 hours.

Sprinkle with the cocoa powder just before serving. Do not sprinkle the cocoa powder on top of the dessert until you're ready to serve, otherwise it will disappear as it dissolves into the cake.

SERVES 8–10

2 organic or free-range eggs, separated
350g mascarpone
60g caster sugar
200ml cold black coffee (don't use instant coffee – use a long espresso)
50ml vin santo (Tuscan dessert wine)
1 teaspoon granulated sugar
250g savoiardi (ladyfinger biscuits)
4 tablespoons unsweetened dark cocoa powder (60–75%)

One way to use up leftover panettone is to cut it into thick fingers for using in tiramisù.

MID-AUGUST HOLIDAY LUNCH

Ferragosto

PRESENT

Family, friends and close relatives

....

ANTIPASTO

Parma ham, melon and fig jam

PASTA

Fettuccine with broccoli, orange, anchovies and Pecorino

MAINS

Sardine casserole

Roast pistachio quails

SIDES

Tomato *peperonata*

DESSERT

Peaches in wine

FERRAGOSTO is a must-do lunch

celebrated with friends and family. The holiday destination of one of the group is chosen and everyone heads there for a summer lunch and an overnight stay, regardless of how far you have to travel. It's *Ferragosto* (the August holiday) as I write and my phone hasn't stop bleeping with messages of *buon Ferragosto* from everyone I know in Italy. I am very fond of this holiday and have so many memories of *Ferragosto* lunches in the Alps, at the beach in Porto San Giorgio and in the Tuscan countryside. Get togethers such as *Ferragosto* make you feel part of something – a family, community, region or country.

When you go to the beach in Italy, you might notice how close everyone sits next to each other. Bars and restaurants are the same – they are either crowded or empty. Should you happen to be the first person or family to arrive at the beach, the next group to arrive will set themselves down quite close to you, even though the beach might stretch for miles. The next to arrive after that will settle close to you on the other side, and everyone who arrives after that will settle nearby, radiating out from where you are sitting until the beach is full. Italians are warm people who enjoy company. There is no such thing as a secret or keeping your problems to yourself. While you might think this is intrusive, in Italy it simply means that people care. It took some time for me to get used to this, but now I really appreciate that people want to be near me and seek out my company. And besides, earwigging in on the conversations nearby can be highly entertaining.

Private beaches are common and families book the same umbrella in the same spot year after year. Children grow up together into adulthood and their children's children will meet under those same umbrellas, playing the Scopa card game, collecting figurine cards from the newspaper vending kiosk, building sandcastles and sharing sandwiches.

Parma ham, melon and fig jam

Prosciutto di Parma, melone e marmelata di fichi

Besides being a delectable combination, Parma ham, melon and fig is perfect for warm, sunny days and balmy evenings. Imagine you are sitting on a white sandy beach under your umbrella. There is a hint of a light breeze and you are staring out at the horizon, where it is impossible to discern where the deep blue sea ends and the sky begins. People are starting to leave the beach. The attendant is closing the umbrellas one by one. Silence descends and the birds arrive, quietly making beautiful webbed prints in the sand. The time is just right for a light antipasto and perhaps a glass of cold, dry white wine.

Alas, I tend to leave the beach looking like something the cat has dragged home. When my children were small, I was not a pretty sight, laden down with plastic bags of various shapes and sizes containing sun creams, toys, towels and togs. I envied Italian women, who after a day at the beach emerged miraculously refreshed, sporting lovely red lipstick, perfectly tanned, moisturised bodies and beautifully groomed hair. Their towels, toys and paraphernalia would be packed into fashionable bags, with their equally well-manicured children in tow. My friend Phyll, who also has a house in the Marche, surmised that because so many Italians live in apartments, they are used to being organised and utilising space efficiently.

Continued overleaf

SERVES 12

2 ripe cantaloupe melons
24 slices of Parma ham or
    prosciutto San Daniele
200g mascarpone

For the fig jam:
2kg ripe figs, left whole
250g muscovado sugar
zest and juice of 1 lemon
1 level teaspoon ground
    cinnamon

Here is the difference between two of my friends, both chic ladies. Imelda, my Irish friend, can never find anything in her LV bag and spends her life looking for the keys of her vintage Mercedes amongst blushers, bracelets, lozenges, lipsticks, perfumes, purses and plenty of invitations to numerous exhibitions. Laura, my Italian friend, who I fondly call Poppins (as in Mary Poppins), has everything perfectly placed in her handbag. Out pops an umbrella when needed, hat, gloves, scarf (wool or silk, depending on the requirement), torch, lighter, Alessi purse hook, vitamins, paracetamol, treats, homeopathic cures, a purse for coins, a purse for business cards and yet another purse for bank notes. I could continue in this vein by comparing my wardrobe to my husband Stefano's, but the less said about that, the better.

TO MAKE THE FIG JAM, place all the ingredients in a heavy-based saucepan and bring to a simmer. Continue to cook on a low heat for 30 minutes. You want to get a thick jam consistency, but at the same time you also want to retain nice big pieces of fruit. Remove from the heat and leave to cool.

Cut each melon into 12 half-moon slices. Cut the flesh away from the hard melon rind.

Drape two slices of Parma ham on 12 plates. Place two slices of melon on each plate and a dollop of mascarpone. Finish with a good helping of fig jam and serve.

Fettuccine with broccoli, orange, anchovies and Pecorino

Fettuccine con broccoli, arance, acciughe e pecorino

An unfaultable summer pasta dish. The fresh oranges just might fool you into thinking you are eating something light.

COOK THE PASTA in a large saucepan of boiling salted water until al dente or according to the packet instructions.

Toast the breadcrumbs in a large, dry pan on a medium heat for a couple of minutes. Remove from the heat and set aside.

Cook the broccoli in a saucepan of boiling salted water for about 5 minutes, just until it's al dente. Drain the broccoli and refresh under cold running water to keep its vibrant green colour. Set aside.

Heat the olive oil in a large pan over a low heat. Sauté the garlic and anchovies for about 1 minute, just until the garlic is fragrant but not browned. Mash the anchovies into the oil with a wooden spoon until they dissolve. Add the broccoli and heat through, then add the oranges and warm for a couple of seconds.

Add the drained pasta to the pan and toss well. Sprinkle with the toasted breadcrumbs and Pecorino shavings. Season to taste with salt and pepper and serve immediately.

SERVES 6

500g fettuccine
30g fresh breadcrumbs
250g broccoli florets
4 tablespoons extra virgin olive oil
2 garlic cloves, crushed
5 tinned anchovies
3 oranges, peeled and cut into cubes
50g Pecorino shavings
salt and freshly ground black pepper

Sardine casserole

Sardine in tegame

Sardines are so very Sicilian – or should I say Aeolian, as those island people think of themselves as neither Italian nor Sicilian. When you talk to someone who has been to the islands, everyone has their favourite: Lipari, Vulcano, Salina, Stromboli, Filicudi, Alicudi and Panarea. My favourite is Salina, with its busy port that is bustling from the early morning to late evening, with fishermen and tourists intermingling at the local bar and boats unloading their passengers laden down with luggage (islands call for long stays). Stefano loves Stromboli, with its threatening volcano spitting fire against the austere black beaches and sheer white cottages. If you are looking for somewhere a little exotic and don't want to travel to the other side of the world, check out the Capofaro resort on Salina for a truly romantic vacation.

PREHEAT THE OVEN to 200°C. Grease a 24cm square ovenproof casserole dish with 4 tablespoons of the olive oil.

Mix the breadcrumbs, pistachios, oregano, parsley, lemon zest and some salt and pepper in a large bowl.

Heat the remaining 8 tablespoons of olive oil in a large pan or wok over a medium heat and fry the sardines, skin side down, in batches just for a minute or two to crisp up the skin. Remove with a slotted spoon and place on a plate lined with kitchen paper to remove the excess oil.

Place a layer of sardines, skin side down, on the bottom of the casserole dish. Sprinkle with the breadcrumbs and dot with olives. Keep layering until all of the ingredients are used up, finishing with a layer of breadcrumbs. Cook in the oven for 10 minutes, until the breadcrumbs are golden and the sardines are cooked through. Serve immediately with chunky lemon wedges.

SERVES 8–10

12 tablespoons extra virgin olive oil
200g fresh breadcrumbs
100g pistachio nuts, shelled and crushed
bunch of fresh oregano or basil
bunch of fresh flat-leaf parsley, roughly chopped
zest of 1 lemon
salt and freshly ground black pepper
1kg fresh sardines, gutted, cleaned and butterflied
200g stoned black Italian olives
lemon wedges, to serve

Use an oven-to-table casserole dish for convenience. I like to add raisins, pistachios and saffron to make it a little Moorish.

Roast pistachio quails

Quaglie pettinate con pistacchi

Your quails must be really fresh – put a word in your butcher's ear to that effect. Crispy-skinned roast quails are irresistible and your guests will probably ask for second helpings.

FIRST PREPARE THE POLENTA. If using instant polenta, make it according to the packet instructions. If using polenta cornmeal, fill a large saucepan with 1½ litres cold water and the salt. Bring the water to a simmer, then gradually add the cornmeal a little at a time. Stir continuously to make sure there are no lumps. It takes 45 minutes to 1 hour to cook the polenta. You may need to add a little warm water if it's looking too dry. The polenta is ready when it comes away easily from the sides of the saucepan.

Preheat the oven to 200°C.

Using a mortar and pestle or a blender, grind together the pistachio nuts, sage leaves and a good pinch of coarse sea salt. Work in 4 tablespoons of the olive oil. Coat the birds inside and out with the paste.

Heat the remaining 4 tablespoons of oil in a large casserole dish over a medium heat. Working in batches, brown the birds lightly all over.

Nestle all the quails in the casserole dish. Roast in the oven for about 30 minutes, basting the birds intermittently, until the skin is nice and crispy. Pierce one of the birds – if the juices run clear, the birds are done.

Serve a whole quail atop a nice portion of runny polenta. Drizzle with a little excellent extra virgin olive oil and serve straightaway. It is impossible to resist pulling the bird apart with your hands and savouring the flesh. Your guests will be licking their fingers.

SERVES 12

50g shelled pistachio nuts
bunch of fresh sage
coarse sea salt
8 tablespoons extra virgin olive oil
12 ready-to-use quails
your best extra virgin olive oil, for drizzling

For the polenta:
1½ litres cold water
1 level tablespoon salt
250g polenta cornmeal or instant polenta
100ml good-quality extra virgin olive oil

Tomato *peperonata*

Peperonata al pomodoro

The smell of *peperonata* cooking always reminds me of summer in Rome. As a working mum living in Trastevere with my young son, Ghinlon, we lived it up when I got paid at the end of each month. We ate out in local restaurants every evening for the first half of the month and survived on more wholesome dishes such as stews, beans, lentils and chickpeas for the second half of the month, all based on recipes dished out by our enthusiastic butcher after consultation with his wife, Gina, who spent a lot of time at the hairdresser.

One of our favourite haunts was Augusto's restaurant, where you were expected to set the table yourself with butcher's paper and plastic-handled cutlery, cut your own bread from huge freshly baked loaves from the *fornaio* (bakery) on Vicolo del Moro and take what you were given – *i piatti del giorno* (plates of the day). The food was genuine and the choice limited: one *primo* pasta dish and one *secondo* (mains). Memories of slow-cooked *coda alla vaccinara* (oxtail), *trippa alla romana* (tripe) and *spezzatino* (beef stew) still linger on my tongue. Wine was dispensed from two welcoming taps protruding from an enormous Formica cabinet, the choice being rough red or bitter white. Augusto was a big, hoarse, bear-like man who never smiled, but secretly he fostered us. He fed half of the students of Rome and ran generous tabs – I'm sure we ate more than we paid for.

Continued overleaf

SERVES 6

6 medium peppers (use a mix of colours)
6 tablespoons extra virgin olive oil
2 medium onions (I prefer red onions), thinly sliced
4 fresh basil leaves
1 teaspoon salt
250ml tomato passata
small sprig of fresh thyme
crusty bread, to serve

The English language cinema, Il Pasquino, was a big attraction and had much more to offer than our small black and white TV, whose hazy reception relied on a manipulated clothes hanger. In summer the Pasquino opened its roof to the stars and a wonderful cool breeze. One very hot summer evening, the neighbours, fed up listening to a foreign language, hurled a cat through the roof. It landed with a piercing screech on top of some poor viewer. No damage done, it hopped off and disappeared out the back door.

A night out wasn't complete without a stop at Marcello's bar in Piazza San Calisto. Ghinlon helped Marcello make the ice cream with fresh eggs, fruit, milk, nuts and cream. In return, we were offered plenty of free ice cream. Marcello, originally from Abruzzo, has been adopted by the Trasteveriani, and although his bar is very basic it offers a home away from home to vendors in the local fruit and vegetable market, artists, writers, artisans and just about anyone else. Thirty years on, I still would not miss an ice cream from Marcello in a small thick glass with fresh cream in the bottom, dark chocolate in the middle and lashings of sweetened fresh cream on top. Marcello's is another *ritrovo* – a welcoming place where I always meet someone I know, whether it's the *portiere* (concierge) of our old building, her daughters and grandchildren, the butcher who called me *stellina* (little star) and insisted I buy the best fillet for my young son, old neighbours or friends.

Deseed the peppers and cut them lengthways into 1cm-wide strips. Rinse under cold running water to make sure no seeds are still clinging to them.

Heat the olive oil in a large pan over a low heat. Fry the onions for about 5 minutes, until they start to soften. Add the peppers, basil and salt to the pan, cover and cook on a low heat for 20 minutes, stirring occasionally.

Add the tomato passata and thyme, cover and cook for 20 minutes more, until the peppers have melted into a thick sauce. Add a little warm water if it looks too dry and stir every now and then. Perfect with fresh crusty bread.

Peaches in wine

Pesche al vino

Peaches in wine is summer in a glass: ripe, juicy peaches and cold white wine, reposing and reflecting.

TO PEEL THE PEACHES, place them in a saucepan of boiling water for 30 seconds. Remove with a slotted spoon and transfer the peaches to a bowl of ice-cold water. Pinch some of the skin with your fingers – it should easily slip off. Once all the peaches have been peeled, cut them into slices.

Place a whole sliced peach in a glass and top up with white wine. Refrigerate for 2 hours. Serve with a dessert fork. Your guests will eat the peaches and then drink the refreshing peach wine.

SERVES 12

12 ripe peaches
2 bottles of cold white wine, such as Pinot Grigio, Pecorino or Vermentino

SACRED SAGRE - STREET FOOD

Le Sagre del Territorio

PRESENT

Townships

....

ON THE MENU

Stuffed green olives

Stuffed courgette flowers

Supplì

Fried calamari

Cheese fritters

SAGRE

are festivals celebrating territorial dishes based on local and seasonal ingredients. While this might sound trendy, Italians have been doing it for hundreds of years. What were once pagan and then religious festivities have evolved into provincial cultural events involving entire townships. Each village has an entertainment committee made up of the local butcher, baker and barista. The onus is on the members to promote the best of local cuisine, provide musical entertainment and raise enough money to fund further festivals.

The Marchigiani (people of the Marche region) probably have the most *sagre* in Italy. Each town and village celebrates everything from cockles, gnocchi, funghi and olives to chestnuts, snails and sauces. When you vacation in the Marche region, there is bound to be an abundance of *sagre* worth checking out. August, although extremely hot, offers unforgettable fêtes involving medieval-style flag throwing, archery, bareback horse racing in 16th-century costume known as *palio* and re-enactments of medieval battles in costume. During the first weekend of August the townspeople of Grottazzolina, wearing medieval attire, open the festival with canon fire salutes. Gigantic medieval playgrounds and stalls selling artisan crafts and foods adorn the village, a festival of colour and smells, and only medieval coinage can be used throughout that weekend. On the last evening there is a sumptuous medieval banquet feast on top of the castle following a superb re-enactment of an ancient battle on horseback. The festival ends with a mesmerising fireworks display. Just bear in mind that you won't get to sleep until the early hours, as the townspeople tend to have a *riposino* (nap) in the long, hot afternoons and are very *allegri* (joyful) from midnight on.

Sagre are also an essential part of the cultural fabric of the Castelli Romani. Frascati, being close to Rome, is where Romans head to on weekends to eat porchetta (roast pork on a spit), enjoy fried foods, which they are particularly fond of, and drink Frascati white wine at communal tables. On one such fine autumn evening, as I sauntered through the town with some difficulty (balancing platform shoes on cobbled stones wasn't an easy feat), I noticed a group of elderly gentlemen playing Neapolitan card games and was drawn by the beautiful depictions on the cards. When the gentlemen spotted my interest, they invited me to join in and offered shot glasses of crisp white Frascati wine, and in no time, with the help of a constant flow of wine, I became a whizz at Scopa, a fast and devious card game. We drew a huge group of supporters and played until midnight. The porchetta was the best I'd ever eaten, the *supplì* were sublime and I unwittingly found a new appreciation for very basic Frascati house wine, the effects of which were so long-lasting that after that adventure, an abstention from alcohol was called for, which lasted 10 years. That is, until I met my Italian husband, Stefano, under whose guidance I developed a more discerning palate. The family's preferred wine is Barbera, since Stefano's mum grew up in Torino. Nonna Valentina always had a small glass of Barbera at lunchtime and another in the evening. The cork would be replaced in the bottle with a sharp slap and pop of the palm and the bottle would be carefully returned to the sideboard, standing to attention, waiting for the next meal.

Stuffed green olives

Olive ascolane

Ascolane olives are a speciality of the beautiful medieval town of Ascoli Piceno in the Marche region. If you happen upon the town, make sure you have coffee in the Caffè Meletti, and a visit to the bathroom is a must – while you wash your hands, you can gaze down through the glass floor at the wonders of the Roman empire lying beneath a medieval layer.

I have eaten stuffed olives all over Italy, and I must say that the ones from Ascoli are the very best. Traditionally a mixture of minced meats is used in the stuffing, but 100 per cent pork works very well. For those who don't eat pork, use half beef and half chicken or turkey, or chicken and pork for who those who don't eat beef.

To make the stuffing, heat the olive oil in a large, wide pan over a medium heat. Make a *soffritto* by frying the onion, carrot and celery for 3 minutes. Add the minced meats and stir until the meat turn a nice deep colour. Pour in the wine and increase the heat momentarily to cook off the alcohol. Remove from the heat and add the rest of the stuffing ingredients. Season with salt and pepper. Mix well and leave to cool.

SERVES 8

1kg plain, large green olives (Ascolane olives are the best variety for this)

For the stuffing:
4 teaspoons extra virgin olive oil
1 small onion, finely diced
1 carrot, peeled and finely diced
1 celery stick, finely diced
100g minced pork
100g minced chicken
100g minced beef
200ml dry white wine
60g freshly grated parmigiano or Pecorino
30g dried Italian breadcrumbs (pangrattato)
1 organic or free-range egg, beaten
pinch of nutmeg
salt and freshly ground black pepper

For the breadcrumb coating:
200g dried Italian breadcrumbs (pangrattato)
100g plain flour
2 organic or free-range eggs, beaten
1 litre nut oil or sunflower oil, for frying

Pit each olive as follows. Place the olive on a chopping board and place a wide knife on top. Press down with pressure and the stone will pop out.

Blitz the stuffing in a blender or food processor to obtain a very fine consistency and place in a piping bag fitted with a nozzle with a large round tip. Fill each pitted olive with the stuffing.

To make the breadcrumb coating, place the breadcrumbs, flour and beaten eggs in three separate shallow bowls. Roll each olive first in the flour, then in the egg and lastly in the breadcrumbs.

Heat the oil in a large saucepan or a deep-fat fryer until it reaches 175°C. Fry the olives in batches until they turn a beautiful light golden colour. Remove with a slotted spoon and place on a plate lined with kitchen paper to remove the excess oil. Eat hot and enjoy. To create an authentic country effect, serve four or five olives per person on squares of brown paper or create paper cones. I like a squeeze of lemon juice, although my Marchigiani friends tell me this is sacrilege.

Stuffed courgette flowers

Fiori di zucca

Stuffed courgette flowers are irresistible and my favourite are ones stuffed with a little ricotta and anchovies. This would be a very posh *sagra* food.

TO MAKE THE FILLING, place the ricotta in a sieve and leave for 1 hour to let the excess liquid drain away. Combine the strained ricotta, parmigiano and lemon zest in a mixing bowl and set aside.

To make the batter, place the flours and a pinch of salt in a large bowl and mix them together. Using a whisk, gradually incorporate the sparkling water. Whisk until it forms a fluid, thick batter with no lumps.

Open the flowers and remove the stamens. Wash gently and pat dry with a clean cotton cloth. Fill each flower with a good tablespoon of the ricotta mixture, then push one anchovy into the middle of the filling. Close over the petals.

Heat the oil in a large saucepan or a deep-fat fryer until it reaches 170°C. Test the oil by dropping a small piece of bread into it. If it sizzles, it's ready. Dip each flower in batter and gently shake off the excess. Fry the flowers in the oil, two at a time, for a couple of minutes, until the flowers turn a lovely light golden colour. Remove with a slotted spoon and transfer to a plate lined with kitchen paper to remove the excess oil.

Keep the flowers warm in a low oven while you cook the rest. Serve immediately.

MAKES 12

200g fresh ricotta

2 tablespoons freshly grated parmigiano

1 teaspoon lemon zest

200g plain flour

100g semolina flour or cornflour

pinch of salt

200ml very cold sparkling water

12 courgette flowers

12 tinned anchovies (optional)

1 litre sunflower oil, for frying

You can fill your courgette flowers with buffalo mozzarella – just don't forget to strain off the excess water first. And since you are in the mood for frying, why not cut the courgettes themselves into 6cm x 1cm batons, dip them in batter and fry to make courgette chips?

Supplì

Supplì are a Roman street food, and while the traditional recipe calls for a rich *ragù* sauce, I prefer a lighter tomato sauce. This recipe is for my nephew Conor Curran. Despite his name, he is thoroughly Italian. He's a devout follower of the Milan football team, he insists on speaking Italian, complete with an abundance of hand gestures, to his bewildered Irish parents and he can spot the best *supplì* wherever we go.

To make the sauce, heat the olive oil in a wide, heavy-based saucepan over a low heat. Sweat the shallots for about 5 minutes, until they are soft and translucent. Place the tinned tomatoes in a bowl and mash them with a fork. Add the mashed tomatoes to the saucepan along with the fresh tomatoes, basil and salt. Stir, cover and cook for 15 minutes. Blend with a hand blender.

Heat the blended tomato sauce to just below simmering, then stir in the hot water, rice and salt. Cover and cook the rice over a low heat, stirring occasionally, for about 15 minutes. At this point the rice should have absorbed all of the sauce. Taste and check if it is cooked – you may need to add a little more warm water and continue cooking the rice for another couple of minutes. Bear in mind that the rice will continue to absorb the moisture of the raw egg when it gets added, so it should be a little al dente.

Remove from the heat and add the parmigiano, butter, two beaten eggs and a pinch of salt. Leave to cool and set for a couple of hours. Alternatively, you could prepare the rice the day before and keep it in the fridge.

MAKES ABOUT 20

500ml hot water

500g Italian superfino rice or Arborio rice

1 heaped teaspoon salt

100g freshly grated parmigiano

50g butter

4 free-range or organic eggs

400g cow's milk mozzarella

500g dried Italian breadcrumbs (pangrattato)

1 litre sunflower oil, for frying

For the tomato sauce:

4 tablespoons extra virgin olive oil

2 shallots, finely sliced

2 x 400g tins of whole plum tomatoes

2 fresh ripe plum tomatoes, chopped

4 fresh basil leaves

1 teaspoon salt

When you're ready to make the *supplì*, cut the mozzarella into 2cm cubes.

Put the breadcrumbs in a shallow bowl and the remaining two beaten eggs in a second shallow bowl. I suggest using transparent deli gloves to keep your hands clean.

Take a portion of rice in the palm of your hand (about the size of two ping pong balls) and mould into an elongated oval shape. Make a dent in the middle and insert a couple cubes of mozzarella. Wrap the rice around the cheese to completely enclose it. Continue until you've used up all the rice and cheese.

Dip each *supplì* in the beaten eggs, shaking off any excess, then coat all over in breadcrumbs.

Heat the oil in a deep, wide saucepan or a deep-fat fryer until it reaches 175°C. Test the temperature of the oil by dropping a small piece of bread in it – if it sizzles, the oil is ready.

Fry two or three *supplì* at a time until they turn a golden brown colour. Remove with a slotted spoon and place on a plate lined with kitchen paper to remove the excess oil. Serve the *supplì* while they're still hot.

Supplì and beer are perfect for football and rugby match gatherings in front of the TV. Try placing an anchovy in the centre alongside the mozzarella, as mozzarella and anchovies are a perfect marriage.

andidati"

ella, trova
azionare"

...nelli non dovrebbero creare pro-

...sinistra per il gol renziano?
...narcazione: «È vero che se
...spero, è un successo po-
...stato e sarà aspro, ma
...po dello Stato». Cuper-
...manescorse. Più cau-
...Vedremo». Gli fa eco
...ntuomo delle isti-
...della minoranza
...tte». Solo Ugo
...anno vinto tut-
...a tirato la vo-
...ono i veltro-
...zi a Palazzo
...escimento
...tag #Ser-
...riforme:
...ambiare».

Congiura

Fried calamari

Calamari fritti

A mandatory finger food, best eaten from a brown paper wrapper with plenty of salt and lemon juice.

To make the batter, place the flours and a pinch of salt in a large bowl and mix them together. Using a whisk, gradually incorporate the sparkling water and the beaten egg yolk. Whisk until it forms a fluid, thick batter with no lumps.

Cut the squid into 1cm-thick circles. Rinse in cold water and pat dry with kitchen paper. Place the calamari rings into the bowl of batter and swirl to ensure they get a good coating.

Heat the oil in a large saucepan or a deep-fat fryer until it reaches 170°C. Test the temperature of the oil by dropping a small piece of bread in it – if it sizzles, the oil is ready.

Using a slotted spoon, scoop up a bunch of calamari, shake off any excess batter and gently drop into the oil to fry. They are ready when the colour changes to a nice golden brown. Remove with a clean slotted spoon and transfer to a plate lined with kitchen paper to remove the excess oil. Serve piping hot with some lemon wedges.

Serves 4

500g fresh squid (ask your fishmonger to clean it and remove the tentacles) or frozen calamari rings, defrosted
1 litre sunflower oil, for frying
3 lemons, cut into wedges

For the batter:
200g plain flour
200g semolina flour or cornflour
pinch of salt
400ml very cold sparkling water
1 free-range or organic egg yolk, beaten

To create a main course such as fritto misto *(fried fish), the process is much the same. Use fresh shelled prawns, ready-to-use fresh sardines and chunks of fresh hake, dip in batter and fry until golden.*

Cheese fritters

Formaggio fritto

Deliciously crunchy on the outside, soft and creamy on the inside.

PREPARE THREE SHALLOW BOWLS: one with flour, one with breadcrumbs and one with the beaten egg yolks.

Coat the cheese cubes first in flour, then egg and then breadcrumbs (keep the bowls for the second coating). Place in the fridge for 1 hour, then repeat the process of coating.

Heat the oil in a large saucepan or deep-fat fryer to 180℃. Test the temperature of the oil by dropping a small piece of bread in it – if it sizzles, the oil is ready.

Fry the cheese fritters for 3–4 minutes, until they turn golden brown. Remove with a slotted spoon and place on a plate lined with kitchen paper to remove the excess oil.

SERVES 6–8

100g plain flour

100g dried Italian breadcrumbs (pangrattato)

3 free-range or organic egg yolks, beaten

400g Fontina cheese, cut into 3cm cubes

1 litre sunflower oil, for frying

The apricot and basil compote on page 202 is a delicious dip for these fritters.

OCTOBER TRUFFLE CELEBRATIONS

Sagra del Tartufo

PRESENT

Townspeople and tourists

....

ANTIPASTO

Tartine with truffle butter

PASTA

Tagliolini with truffle and anchovies

MAINS

Tagliata of beef with truffle

SIDES

Pan-fried chantarelle mushrooms with truffle

THE BEST time to visit Alba, a culinary paradise, is during

the month of October. The streets are lined with mere tents housing truffle stalls majestically called 'sitting rooms of tastes and scents'. Vendors sit like aristocratic jewellers guarding their precious wares. Wonderful Barolo, Dolcetto, Barbaresco, Nebbiolo and Gavi di Gavi wines are offered to wash down small plates of truffle delights.

Tartine with truffle butter

Tartine con burro tartufato

Good butter embedded with truffle on hot bread is glorious.

PREPARE THE TRUFFLE by rinsing it quickly and lightly brushing off any dirt. Grate finely and whip with the softened butter.

Toast the bread on both sides. Remove the crust and spread with the truffle butter. Cut each slice into four pieces and serve straightaway.

MAKES 12

1 x 20g truffle
200g butter, softened
3 long, thick slices of crusty bread

Truffle butter can be whisked into risottos or used to finish off pasta dishes. It's also used in the recipe for tagliata of beef with truffle on page 244.

Tagliolini with truffle and anchovies

Tagliolini con tartufo e acciughe

Tagliolini pasta is just right for truffles. The pasta is fine and doesn't impede the unique truffle flavour.

COOK THE PASTA in a large saucepan of boiling salted water until al dente or according to the packet instructions. Reserve a ladleful of the cooking water before you drain the pasta.

Heat the olive oil in a large pan over a low heat. Sauté the anchovies and garlic for about 1 minute, just until the garlic is fragrant but not browned. Mash the anchovies into the oil with a wooden spoon until they dissolve. Remove the garlic with a slotted spoon and discard, then stir in the chilli flakes. Add the reserved cooking water from the pasta to the pan.

Prepare the truffle by rinsing it quickly and lightly brushing off any dirt. Slice with a truffle slicer or mandoline or as thinly as possible with your sharpest knife.

Add the drained pasta to the pan and mix well. Remove from the heat and fold in the freshly sliced truffles. Serve immediately.

SERVES 6–8

500g tagliolini egg pasta

4 tablespoons extra virgin olive oil

4 salted anchovies

2 garlic cloves, peeled and left whole

¼ teaspoon dried chilli flakes

1 x 20g truffle

Pan-fried chantarelle mushrooms with truffle

Finferli in padella con tartufo

Finferli and truffle, jewels of the forest.

HEAT THE OLIVE OIL in a large pan over a low heat. Sauté the garlic for about 1 minute, just until it's fragrant but not browned. Remove with a slotted spoon and discard. Add the mushrooms and a pinch of salt to the oil, cover the pan and cook for 10 minutes.

Prepare the truffle by rinsing it quickly and lightly brushing off any dirt. Slice with a truffle slicer, a mandoline or as thinly as possible using your sharpest knife. Add the sliced truffles to the mushrooms, season to taste with salt and serve warm.

SERVES 4

4 tablespoons extra virgin olive oil

2 garlic cloves, peeled and left whole

200g chantarelle mushrooms, left whole

salt

1 x 20g truffle

Serve the mushrooms with fillet of beef, to dress some tagliolini pasta or more simply on a bruschetta of toasted bread.

Tagliata of beef with truffle

Tagliata di manzo con tartufo

This is pure decadence: good steak, truffle and creamy butter.

PREPARE THE TRUFFLES by rinsing them quickly and lightly brushing off any dirt.

Toss the rocket leaves in the extra virgin olive oil.

Heat a griddle pan until it's smoking hot. Brush the steaks with a little olive oil. Cook the steaks, two at a time, for 3 minutes on each side. Finish with a knob of truffle butter and a pinch of salt. Set the steaks aside to rest.

Cut each striploin into four or five pieces. Slice the truffles with a truffle slicer or mandoline or as thinly as possible with your sharpest knife.

Place a bed of the dressed rocket on warmed plates. Top with slices of steak and freshly cut truffles.

SERVES 6

2 x 20g truffles
bunch of fresh rocket
2 tablespoons extra virgin olive oil
6 x 150g striploin steaks
knob of truffle butter (page 241)
salt

ALL SAINTS AND SOULS DAYS

Tutti i Santi e il Giorno dei Morti

PRESENT
Family, friends and close older relatives

....

ANTIPASTO
Dumplings in capon broth

PASTA
Pappardelle with braised wild boar *stracotto*

MAINS
Rabbit and chicken casserole

SIDES
Pan-fried butternut squash and oregano

DESSERT
Ricotta and cherry tart

Caprese flourless chocolate cake

IL GIORNO *dei Santi* (All Saints Day) is a reflective day prior to the *Giorno dei Morti* (All Souls Day). One might pay homage to a favourite saint, but mostly it's a time spent dwelling on departed family members.

Il Giorno dei Morti is a day when Italians visit the graves not only of their own loved ones, but even more endearingly they place flowers on the neglected graves that don't have visitors. It's actually quite exciting for children to wake up early and accompany the adults to the *fioraio* (flower shop) to buy masses of flowers, then take them home and create little bundles tied up with colourful ribbons. Then there is the playful search around the graveyard looking for graves with no flowers and the sense of benevolence and curiosity on bestowing those beautiful bundles on unmarked or neglected tombs. Graveyards are packed with visitors and there can be major traffic jams around the large ones, especially on the outskirts of cities. Chrysanthemums are the most common grave flowers, so never bring a bunch of chrysanthemums to an Italian household. It's considered bad luck and you won't be allowed to pass the threshold.

When Stefano's father passed away we flew over from Ireland and headed for the hospital. We asked to see Giorgio and were given instructions on where he was to be found in the morgue. We tearfully made our way along the cold, fluorescent-lit, insipid pale green corridors, a perfect match for our mood. Pushing open a big, heavy door, we found Giorgio perfectly at peace, elegantly dressed in his finest attire and in the company of four elderly and lovely country women who were laid out in the room with him. The ladies, sporting identical hairstyles – small grey buns drawn tightly to the nape of the neck – were dressed identically too in paisley shirts buttoned up to the collar, neatly buttoned black or navy short cardigans, three-quarter-length black synthetic skirts, thick brown tights and laced black shoes. It was a totally unexpected and surreal moment. We looked at each other, smiled and left, comforted in the knowledge that Giorgio wasn't alone.

Dumplings in capon broth

Canederli in brodo di cappone

Italians are very good at using every last morsel, creating something new, nutritious and delicious from something old. This is an intriguing way to use up stale bread, but it should be good bread. I don't suggest using sliced pan, but rather a leftover piece of sourdough or a good crusty loaf. Dumplings are classic comfort food, and is there anything more comforting than a good capon broth?

To make the capon broth, fill a pot with 2 litres of cold water. Add all of the broth ingredients and bring to the boil. Cover, reduce the heat and simmer for 2 hours. Leave to cool, then skim off all the fat and strain the ingredients. Remove the meat from the capon and discard the skin and bones. Shred the meat into small pieces and return it to the broth.

To make the dumplings, place the breadcrumbs in a bowl, cover with the milk and leave for 10 minutes.

Heat a little extra virgin olive oil or a knob of butter in a large pan over a medium heat. Fry the diced onions for about 10 minutes, until softened.

Continued overleaf

Serves 6

For the dumplings:
250g stale bread, whizzed into breadcrumbs
100ml milk
extra virgin olive oil or a knob of butter
1 small onion, diced
1 free-range or organic egg, beaten
1 tablespoon chopped fresh flat-leaf parsley
1 tablespoon chopped fresh chives
1 teaspoon orange zest (optional)
salt and freshly ground black pepper
50g freshly grated parmigiano

For the capon broth:
2 litres cold water
1 medium capon
2 onions, peeled and left whole
2 carrots
2 celery sticks
1 bay leaf
1 tablespoon sea salt
freshly ground black pepper

Squeeze the excess milk out of the breadcrumbs and place the breadcrumbs in a mixing bowl. Add the onions, beaten egg, parsley, chives, orange zest (if using) and some salt and pepper and mix well. Cover with cling film and leave to rest in the fridge for 1 hour.

Place the strained broth and shredded meat in a saucepan and bring back up to a simmer.

Pinch off a little dumpling mixture and roll it between the palms of your hands to form balls the size of a small mandarin. Drop the dumplings in batches of four into the simmering broth for about 10 minutes, until they float to the top.

To serve, ladle the broth into pasta bowls along with a couple of dumplings. Sprinkle with freshly grated parmigiano and a grinding of black pepper.

Pappardelle with braised wild boar *stracotto*

Pappardelle con stracotto di cinghiale

One of the best dishes from Tuscany is wild boar *stracotto*. I recommend young boar to facilitate the cooking. If your butcher only has mature boar, then you need to marinate it for 12 hours or so – use the marinade recipe for the hare sauce on page 116. Wild boar *stracotto* is perfect for cold winter evenings dining in front of a blazing fire and calls for a glass of full-bodied red wine.

MAKE A *SOFFRITTO* by heating the olive oil in a large saucepan over a low heat. Add the diced onion, carrot and celery and sauté for 5 minutes. Add the wild boar pieces and seal the meat. Pour in the wine and increase the heat momentarily to cook off the alcohol.

Place the tomatoes in a bowl and mash them with a fork, then add them to the pan along with the bay leaves and rosemary and season with salt and pepper. Cover and cook for 3 hours over a low heat, until the meat is tender. Add a little warm water if it looks like it's too dry.

Cook the pasta in a large saucepan of boiling salted water until al dente or according to the packet instructions. Drain the pasta and mix the pasta and sauce together in a large serving bowl.

Sprinkle with freshly grated Pecorino (if using) and a grinding of black pepper and serve immediately.

SERVES 6

6 tablespoons extra virgin olive oil
1 medium onion, diced
1 carrot, peeled and diced
1 celery stick, diced
1kg wild young boar suitable for stewing, diced into 3cm pieces
250ml full-bodied red wine
2 x 400g tins of whole plum tomatoes
2 bay leaves
sprig of fresh rosemary
salt and freshly ground black pepper
500g pappardelle pasta
50g freshly grated Pecorino cheese (optional)

Try polenta with stracotto. Cook the polenta as outlined on page 218. Pour the polenta onto a large serving board, such as a pastry board, pour over the stracotto sauce, sprinkle with freshly grated parmigiano or Pecorino and freshly ground black pepper and serve straight to the table.

Rabbit and chicken casserole

Pollo e coniglio alla cacciatora

Many of our guests who are reluctant to eat rabbit are won over when they try the combination of chicken and rabbit. I must confess that I do enjoy eating rabbit. Driving through the Tuscan countryside returning from the Etruscan ruins of Volterra, I couldn't resist an inviting handwritten sign tied around a huge chestnut tree saying 'rabbits and chickens for sale' and I veered onto a meandering dry, white road that took me to a working farmhouse. I say working farmhouse as opposed to a picturesque farmhouse. This farmhouse was surrounded by machinery, spare tractor parts, used tyres, reels of chicken wire, abandoned cars and bathtubs, and numerous dogs and mischievous cats. The farmer and his wife greeted me in the local dialect with an abundance of hand gestures and instructed me to follow them to the rear of the house, where they held up two beautiful, fluffy, long-eared rabbits that were very much alive and kicking. They would be killed and skinned instantly, so which one did I want?

I reluctantly chose the brown rabbit and the farmer took it aside while his lovely wife, Gaetana, noting my disquietude, invited me back to the house. A long wooden latticed table was set for lunch and immediately a third place was set for me. I shared their meal of rabbit casserole and pan-fried peppers, accompanied by huge chunks of casareccio bread that had been baked that morning in the village communal oven.

Continued overleaf

SERVES 8

1 rabbit, skinned and cut into 8 pieces

1 free-range or organic chicken, skinned and cut into 8 pieces

plain flour, for coating

6 tablespoons extra virgin olive oil

4 tinned anchovies

3 garlic cloves, peeled and left whole

2 bay leaves

sprig of fresh rosemary

1 level teaspoon dried chilli flakes

100ml balsamic vinegar or wine vinegar

100g stoned black olives

200ml tomato passata

100ml warm water

pinch of salt

When I eventually left I was given three parcels. One was my fresh rabbit, a sprig of rosemary and a lemon, one was a chunk of cheese, a bottle of homemade wine and plenty of ripe plums and the third was a bucketful of memories from that day.

LIGHTLY COAT THE RABBIT and chicken pieces with flour.

Heat the olive oil in a wide, heavy-based saucepan over a low heat. Sauté the anchovies, garlic, bay leaves and rosemary sprig for about 1 minute, just until the garlic is fragrant but not browned. Mash the anchovies with a wooden spoon until they dissolve, then stir in the chilli flakes.

Working in batches, add the rabbit and chicken pieces and brown them all over. Add the vinegar and increase the heat momentarily. Stir in the olives, tomato passata, warm water and a pinch of salt. Cover and cook over a low heat for 1½ hours, until the meat is tender. Stir regularly and add a little more warm water if it looks too dry. Ladle into warm bowls making sure everyone gets nice pieces of both chicken and rabbit.

Pan-fried butternut squash and oregano

Zucca in padella con origano

Oregano tends to be overused in Italian recipes, but in fact it's not widely used outside of Sicily and Sardinia. The freshly harvested herb is so much nicer and milder than the industrial dried version. My advice is to leave it out of a dish altogether if you can't get hold of a decent fresh bunch.

HEAT THE OIL in a wide, heavy-based saucepan over a medium heat. Add the diced squash and oregano. Cover and cook for 15 minutes, stirring occasionally. The squash should be crisp on the outside and soft on the inside. Season with salt and pepper to taste.

SERVES 4

50ml extra virgin olive oil

1 medium butternut squash, peeled and diced into 1cm cubes

2 tablespoons fresh oregano or thyme

salt and freshly ground black pepper

This is delicious served with a dollop of mascarpone and toasted fingers of bread.

Ricotta and cherry tart

Torta di ricotta e amarene

Ricotta features in a lot of Italian recipes, both savoury and sweet. Grocery stores sell cow's milk ricotta and sheep's milk ricotta, and my favourite is the sheep's milk version. When you consider how mountainous Italy is – home to the great Dolomites of the north and the Apennines running down Italy's spine – you can understand how mountainous communities came to rely heavily on dairy. *Torta di ricotta*, a Roman Jewish speciality, is one of my favourite cakes. It's the kind of cake you cannot resist. You will find yourself returning to the kitchen for another little slice.

To make the filling, strain the cherries and cut them in half. Place all of the filling ingredients except the pine nuts in a bowl and mix together well. Cover the bowl with cling film and refrigerate for half an hour.

Preheat the oven to 180℃. Grease a 23cm circular baking tin.

Cream the butter and sugar together. Add the egg yolk and lemon zest (if using) and mix well. Mix in the flour, then tip the dough out onto a lightly floured board and knead lightly to form a soft dough. Place in a bowl, cover with cling film and refrigerate for half an hour.

Serves 8–10

For the filling:
50g tinned Amarena cherries
400g ricotta cheese
200g caster sugar
2 free-range or organic eggs, beaten
1 free-range or organic egg yolk, beaten, for glazing
zest of 1 orange
zest of 1 lemon
20g pine nuts

For the pastry:
100g butter, softened
100g caster sugar
1 free-range or organic egg yolk, beaten
1 level teaspoon lemon zest (optional)
200g plain flour, plus extra for dusting

Lightly dust a pastry board with flour. Take a little more than half of the dough and roll it out thinly. Line the greased baking tin with the pastry (you can blind bake it if you wish, but it's not necessary).

Toast the pine nuts on a hot, dry pan for 30 seconds, taking care not to let them burn. Fill the lined tin with the ricotta filling and sprinkle over the pine nuts.

Roll out the remaining pastry thinly. Using a sharp knife, cut it into 1.5cm-wide strips that are long enough to cross the top of the tart. Create a criss-cross lattice pattern over the top of the tart with the pastry strips. Seal the edges and glaze the top of the pastry strips with a little beaten egg.

Bake for 25 minutes, until the pastry is golden and the ricotta has set. Serve at room temperature or cold.

You can replace the Amarena cherries with raisins that have been soaked in your favourite liquor or chocolate drops.

Caprese flourless chocolate cake

Torta di ciocolata senza farina o Torta caprese

The island of Capri is a secretive and exotic corner of Europe, a place that everyone knows about but perhaps it seems too iconic to merit a visit. While there is some inherent truth to this, such as the high street of super-chic boutiques and luxurious hotels, at the same time the island can be captivatingly charming.

If a dessert can be called sinful, it's the local Caprese dark chocolate cake, perfect with vanilla ice cream on a hot summer day sitting on a terrace decked with mesmerisingly beautiful turquoise *maioliche* tiles mirrored in a deep blue sea.

PREHEAT THE OVEN to 175℃. Grease a 24cm springform tin.

Break the chocolate into small pieces and place in a stainless steel or heatproof bowl set over a pot of simmering water until it melts. Make sure the bottom of the bowl doesn't touch the water.

Separate the egg whites and yolks. Beat the egg yolks in a small bowl. In a separate spotlessly clean, dry bowl, whip the whites until they form stiff peaks. Gently fold in 100g of the sugar.

Cream the butter and the remaining 100g of the sugar to a creamy consistency. Add the egg yolks and mix again until they are well incorporated. Stir in the ground almonds and melted chocolate, then fold in the sweetened egg whites.

Pour the batter into the greased tin. Bake in the oven for about 1 hour, until a skewer inserted in the centre of the cake comes out clean. Leave to rest for 10 minutes in the tin, then release the cake and cool on a wire rack. This cake is delicious served warm with whipped cream or a scoop of vanilla ice cream and a few fresh rasberries. It can be kept for up to four days in an airtight container and warmed for 30 seconds in a microwave before serving.

SERVES 8–10

250g good-quality dark chocolate

5 free-range or organic eggs, separated

200g caster sugar

250g butter, softened

300g ground almonds

whipped cream or vanilla ice cream, to serve

fresh rasberries, to serve

SKI SUPPER

Spuntino Serale Dopo lo Sci

PRESENT

Friends

....

MENU

Polenta with sausages and mushrooms
Polenta crostini with Swiss chard and Gorgonzola
Polenta gratin with speck and Asiago

MY AUNT Sheila married a man from Trentino, Maurizio Bolner.

His surname, Bolner, is indicative of the history of the area, which has bounced back and forth between Italy and Austria. German and Italian are spoken in these valleys and the cuisine reflects both the Italian and Austrian influences.

When Maurizio settled down with Sheila, a diehard feminist, he soon realised he was expected to host, entertain and educate her numerous family members according to Irish tradition, including nieces, nephews, sisters, brothers, old aunts and in-laws. He diligently purchased a white Transit van to convey the frequent visitors the length and breadth of Italy. As a student I was readily available to go along on these exciting excursions, such as the time we headed off with my sisters to the fashionable ski resort of Madonna di Campiglio close to Maurizio's hometown. Decked out in our second-hand skiing suits (much to Maurizio's indignation) bought at rock-bottom prices from the Porta Portese Sunday flea market, we arrived only to encounter very long queues for the ski lifts.

Now I grew up in an intensely industrialised part of Dublin close to the national gas company, which extracted gas from coal. We children loved the winters when it snowed because those ugly black coal heaps were transformed into our very own snow-white Dolomites. We gathered plastic bags and bits of cardboard and passed the days 'snowboarding' down the snow-covered coal mounds. So to break the monotony of queuing I suggested to Sheila that I could teach her 'snowboarding', and all that was required was a black plastic bag. Dublin girls are felinely mischievous, and my sisters and I prepped her for the experience. We sat her on a plastic bag at the top of a somewhat steep hill, gave her a good push and away she went, zooming along like a torpedo. By the time she came to a stop we realised our misdemeanour and scarpered.

That evening she tracked us down and showed us her multicoloured bruises, an interesting spectrum of mauve, black, purple, yellow and orange, covering the better part of her lower body. I suggested she might cool the bruises with some snow. This was not what she wanted to hear, so we took to our heels and found refuge in the nearby wood cabin restaurant, aptly called a *rifugio* (shelter). We shared a hearty board of polenta with a meaty tomato sauce, washed down with a couple glasses of local Marzemino, the perfect antithesis to the exploits of the day. We finished with a shot of grappa and were ready for a midnight adventure on the piste.

Polenta with sausages and mushrooms

Polenta con salsiccia e funghi

A hearty plate of polenta, sausages and mushrooms in a wood cabin mountain retreat boasting a blazing log fire offers a satisfying end to a vigorous day on the slopes.

HEAT THE OLIVE OIL in a wide, heavy-based saucepan over a medium heat. Fry the onion for about 5 minutes, until it becomes translucent. Add the sausages and cook for 1 minute, then add the mushrooms. Pour in the wine and increase the heat momentarily to cook off the alcohol.

Place the tomatoes in a bowl and mash them with a fork. Add to the saucepan along with the basil, thyme and some salt and pepper. Cover and cook over a low heat for 1 hour.

Meanwhile, make the polenta. If using instant polenta, prepare it according to the packet instructions. If using polenta cornmeal, fill a large saucepan with 1 litre of cold water and the salt. Bring the water to a simmer, then gradually add the cornmeal a little at a time. Stir continuously to make sure there are no lumps. Share the task of stirring, as it takes 45 minutes to 1 hour to cook the polenta. You may need to add a little warm water if it's looking too dry. The polenta is ready when it comes away easily from the sides of the saucepan.

Pour the polenta onto a large serving plate or wooden board, such as a pastry board, and pour over the sauce. Sprinkle generously with freshly grated Pecorino or parmigiano and freshly ground black pepper. Drizzle over a good glug of your best extra virgin olive oil for sheer pleasure. Take your board to the table to create a theatrical atmosphere and everyone can help themselves.

SERVES 6

For the sausage and mushroom sauce:
4 tablespoons extra virgin olive oil
1 onion, thinly sliced
500g fresh Italian salsiccia sausage
250g wild mushrooms
150ml red wine
2 x 400g tins of whole plum tomatoes
small bunch of fresh basil
small sprig of fresh thyme
salt and freshly ground black pepper
100g freshly grated Pecorino or parmigiano
your best extra virgin olive oil, for drizzling

For the polenta:
1 litre cold water
1 teaspoon salt
250g polenta cornmeal or instant polenta

Leftover polenta can be cut into bite-size morsels, fingers or triangles. Fry in really good olive oil or grill to heat it through. Serve with a variety of toppings, such as grilled peppers, broccoli, melted cheese and speck or mozzarella and anchovies.

Polenta crostini with Swiss chard and Gorgonzola

Crostini di polenta con bieta e Gorgonzola

Polenta crostini is an elegant appetiser on a cool autumnal evening with bubbly Prosecco.

IF USING INSTANT POLENTA, prepare it according to the packet instructions. If using polenta cornmeal, fill a large saucepan with 1 litre of cold water and the salt. Bring the water to a simmer, then gradually add the cornmeal a little at a time. Stir continuously to make sure there are no lumps. Share the task of stirring, as it takes 45 minutes to 1 hour to cook the polenta. You may need to add a little warm water if it's looking too dry. The polenta is ready when it comes away easily from the sides of the saucepan.

Tip the polenta onto a serving plate or a large wooden board, such as a pastry board. Leave to cool. When it has cooled and firmed up, cut into thick fingers or triangles.

Immerse the Swiss chard in a saucepan of boiling salted water for 10 minutes. Drain very well and chop.

Heat the olive oil in a large pan over a low heat. Sauté the garlic for about 1 minute, just until it's fragrant but not browned. Add the Swiss chard and cook for a couple of minutes to heat it through.

Spread a little cooked Swiss chard on top of each polenta finger or triangle. Dot with some crumbled Gorgonzola and serve.

SERVES 12

1 litre cold water

1 teaspoon salt

250g polenta cornmeal or instant polenta

500g Swiss chard

4 tablespoons extra virgin olive oil

2 garlic cloves, thinly sliced

250g Gorgonzola, crumbled

Serve warm with an extra glug of good olive oil to get the best results. A crushed hazelnut topping adds a touch of richness.

Polenta gratin with speck and Asiago

Polenta gratinata con speck e Asiago

You might offer your guests small ramekins of polenta gratin as a starter or make a big casserole of gratin for a main course served with spinach with fried garlic and chilli. Children love polenta and it has always been my daughter Aislinn's favourite, which is fortunate since she must eat gluten-free food.

IF USING INSTANT POLENTA, prepare it according to the packet instructions. If using polenta cornmeal, fill a large saucepan with 1 litre of cold water and the salt. Bring the water to a simmer, then gradually add the cornmeal a little at a time. Stir continuously to make sure there are no lumps. Share the task of stirring, as it takes 45 minutes to 1 hour to cook the polenta. You may need to add a little warm water if it's looking too dry. The polenta is ready when it comes away easily from the sides of the saucepan. When it's ready, add in the speck and Asiago.

Preheat the oven to 200°C.

Divide the polenta between 12 small ramekins. Finish off each ramekin with a little freshly grated parmigiano and a knob of butter. Place the 12 ramekins on a baking tray and put in the oven. Keep a close eye on them and remove from the oven when the tops are golden brown, which should take about 15 minutes. Leave to rest for 5 minutes before serving.

MAKES 12 SMALL RAMEKINS

1 litre cold water

1 teaspoon salt

250g polenta cornmeal or instant polenta

200g speck, pancetta or a good cooked ham, thinly sliced and cut into strips

200g Asiago cheese, cut into small cubes

200g freshly grated parmigiano

100g butter

There are any number of tasty combinations you could try, such as cooked ham and mozzarella, peas and Provolone cheese, pistachio, leeks and saffron (add the saffron while cooking the polenta) or truffle and Pecorino. Experiment and discover your own family favourites.

CHRISTMAS EVE DINNER

La Vigilia di Natale

PRESENT

Family and friends

....

ANTIPASTI

Swordfish carpaccio with capers

Tuna tartare with citrus dressing and a shot of Vov

Vov

PASTA

Tonnarelli with shellfish

Wholemeal fettuccine with spinach, potato and anchovy sauce

FISH MAINS

Sea trout parcels

Hake with hazelnut and sage crust

SIDES

Speckled sprouts and leeks

Carrots with parmigiano cream

DESSERT

Christmas cake

THERE'S an Italian saying that goes, *Natale con i tuoi e pasqua con chi vuoi* – Christmas with family and Easter with whomever. It sums up the importance of celebration and family. Christmas consists of three to four days of incessant celebratory eating, but the most important meal is on Christmas Eve. In northern Italy the festive dinner is celebrated with a range of sumptuous meat-based dishes, such as slow-cooked game and polenta, while from the coast of Rome down to Sicily, Christmas Eve dinner is predominantly fish, fish and more fish.

Orders are placed with the fishmonger a month beforehand with strict instructions on just how each element of the order should be gutted, cut, filleted and packed. Recipes have been discussed in minute detail with everyone from neighbours to family and colleagues. Preparation is intense and communal, involving several family members, and the unveiling of the fish dinner is spectacular. While I have selected my favourite dishes encompassing *mare e monti* (sea and mountains), Christmas Eve just has to be fish.

My first Christmas with the family was a unique experience. I was propelled into a matriarchal world of strongly opinionated women, each one charged with guarding the secret recipe of a particular family dish, never to be disclosed. Nonna Valentina created a sublime tuna tartare, mayonnaise and homemade Vov, Auntie Anna prepared heavenly fish sauce, Silvana, my mother-in-law, made stuffed vegetable creations, Annarella (young Anna) transformed hake, sea bream and monkfish into delectable morsels and Francesca created sinfully delicious desserts. What was the price of admittance, you might ask? A huge amount of respect, a touch of humility and an abundance of patience, and in time all was revealed.

Swordfish carpaccio with capers

Carpaccio di pesce con salsina di capperi

Swordfish is synonymous with the Sicilian fish markets of Vucciria, Ballarò and Carlo Alberto. Hectic and noisy, the markets are like a Hieronymus Bosch circus of wild fishmongers vigorously vending their wares, complete with enormous carcasses of swordfish sawn into the thickest cutlets, baskets, boards and blood baths brilliant against sparkling white ice.

SLICE THE SWORDFISH as thinly as possible with your sharpest knife.

Make a marinade of the olive oil, capers, lemon juice and salt and pepper. Use a pestle and mortar to mash everything together.

Put the swordfish slices in a large dish and pour the marinade over. Cover with cling film and put in the freezer for 1 hour, then move to the fridge for a couple of hours.

Lay slices of the marinated swordfish on a large serving plate. Serve with toasted ciabatta or a good country loaf.

SERVES 6

600g fresh swordfish
6 tablespoons extra virgin olive oil
4 tablespoons capers
juice of 3 lemons
salt and freshly ground black
    pepper
toasted ciabatta or crusty bread, to
    serve

An extra splash of your best extra virgin olive oil just before serving would be appreciated.

Tuna tartare with citrus dressing and a shot of Vov

Tartare di tonno agli agrumi con bicchierino di Vov

Thankfully, *La Mattanza*, a traditional Sicilian way of capturing tuna, has been almost phased out. The festivities surrounding the capturing of tuna are akin to the bullfights of Spain. The antique methodology involved capturing migrating tuna during the months of May and June off the western coast of Sicily. These giant bluefin tuna were lured through a series of fishing nets into a zone called *la camera della morte* (the death chamber), where they were brutally slaughtered. I am happy to report that this unsustainable and beastly form of fishing is fading, but hopefully the colourful festivities related to the fresh tuna season will continue.

Tuna tartare is fresh and light and is one of my favourite antipasti. The citrus dressing stimulates the appetite, so it's a good starter for either a meat or fish dinner. A small shot of Vov served with your tuna tartare is a nice surprise for your guests.

DICE THE TUNA into 1cm cubes.

Create an emulsion by whisking together the olive oil, orange and lemon zest and juice, fennel fronds and some salt and pepper in a large bowl.

Add the diced tuna and mix gently to coat the fish with the emulsion. Place in the freezer for 1 hour, then move to the fridge until it's time to serve.

Divide the mixture between 12 small ramekins and serve with breadsticks and a shot of Vov.

SERVES 12

600g fresh line-caught yellowfin tuna
6 tablespoons extra virgin olive oil
zest and juice of 1 orange
zest and juice of 1 lemon
small bunch of fennel fronds
salt and freshly ground black pepper
breadsticks, to serve
Vov shots (overleaf), to serve

Vov

Nonna Valentina made her own Vov, which she was excessively proud of and kept in a beautiful hand-painted bottle. She would recount in minute detail the provenance of the ingredients: the milk and eggs from a farmer near Alba, the Marsala from a small *enoteca* in the centre of Turin. Year in and year out, she never tired of repeating the recipe. Nonno Fernando would try to tell her that we all knew the recipe by now. 'Fernando, it's important,' she would say, smacking his hand. How right she was. Each year now when we make the Vov we think of her and those wonderful dinners. Although Giorgio, Silvana, Valentina and Fernando are no longer with us, their stories and rituals continue to grace our table. So if you want a place at the table of eternity, start cooking.

PLACE THE MILK in a heavy-based saucepan. Split the vanilla pod in half lengthways and scrape the seeds into the milk. Gently heat the milk and vanilla. Remove from the heat just before it reaches the simmering point and leave to cool.

In a large bowl, vigorously whisk the egg yolks and sugar until it's thick and frothy. Gradually whisk in the alcohol and Marsala, then leave to rest for 10 minutes. Stir in the warm milk a little at a time.

Pour into a bottle and refrigerate for up to three days. Sieve before serving in shot glasses.

MAKES 1 LITRE

500ml full-fat milk
1 vanilla pod
5 free-range or organic egg yolks
400g caster sugar
100ml pure alcohol or vodka
100ml Marsala

Tonnarelli with shellfish

Tonnarelli allo scoglio

Having a reliable fishmonger makes cooking so much easier. Your local fishmonger will clean, cut and order in the best fish for you. Nowadays good supermarkets have state-of-the-art fish counters staffed by trained fishmongers, so don't be shy in telling them just how you want your fish gutted, skinned, scaled and cut.

RINSE THE MUSSELS in cold water and pull off the beards. Tap any open mussels on the side of a plate or the counter, and if they don't close, discard them. Steep in plenty of cold water for at least 1 hour and change the water several times.

Steep the clams in a basin of cold water and change the water several times. Tap any open clams on the side of a plate or the counter, and if they don't close, discard them.

To cook the mussels, heat 4 tablespoons of olive oil in a large saucepan over a low heat. Sauté two garlic cloves and ½ teaspoon of the chilli flakes for about 1 minute, just until the garlic is fragrant but not browned. Add the mussels and one-third of the wine and increase the heat momentarily to cook off the alcohol. Add the hot water, cover and cook for a few minutes, until the mussels have opened. Discard any unopened mussels. Strain the juice and set it aside.

Continued overleaf

1kg fresh mussels

400g clams

12 tablespoons extra virgin olive oil

6 garlic cloves, peeled and left whole

1 teaspoon dried chilli flakes

200ml white wine

100ml hot water

500g tonnarelli pasta

200g fresh prawns, shelled

zest of 1 lemon (optional)

12 cherry tomatoes, halved

bunch of fresh flat-leaf parsley,
    finely chopped

To cook the clams, heat 4 tablespoons of olive oil in a large saucepan over a low heat. Sauté one garlic clove and the remaining ½ teaspoon chilli flakes for about 1 minute, just until the garlic is fragrant but not browned. Add the clams and one-third of the wine and increase the heat momentarily to cook off the alcohol. Return to a low heat, cover and cook for a couple of minutes, until all the clams have opened. Discard any unopened clams. Strain the juice and set aside.

Cook the pasta in a large saucepan of boiling salted water until al dente or according to the packet instructions.

While the pasta is cooking, heat 4 tablespoons of olive oil in a large saucepan over a low heat. Sauté the remaining three garlic cloves for about 1 minute, just until the garlic is fragrant but not browned. Stir in the prawns, lemon zest (if using) and the remaining wine and increase the heat momentarily to cook off the alcohol. Return to a low heat. Add the tomatoes, cover and cook for a couple of minutes. Add the mussels and clams along with their strained juices and bring to a simmer, then remove from the heat.

Drain the pasta and add it to the saucepan with the seafood. Give everything a good stir, sprinkle with the chopped parsley and serve immediately.

Remember to put a big bowl on the table for empty shells. The melodious clatter of the empty shells hitting the bowl heightens the merriment at the table.

Wholemeal fettuccine with spinach, potato and anchovy sauce

Fettuccine integrali con spinaci, patate e salsa di acciughe

Potatoes and pasta may not sound quite right, but if the potatoes are cut into tiny cubes and cooked with a nice bite, they engage wonderfully well with pasta and anchovies.

CUT THE POTATOES into small cubes. Cook in a small saucepan of boiling salted water for about 10 minutes, until cooked but still firm. Drain and set aside.

Cook the spinach in boiling water for a couple of minutes. Drain well and set aside.

Whizz the anchovies, garlic and olive oil in a blender to create an emulsion.

Gently warm the cream in a wide, heavy-based saucepan. Fold in the anchovy emulsion, followed by the spinach and potatoes.

Meanwhile, cook the pasta in a large saucepan of boiling salted water until al dente or according to the packet instructions.

Toss the pasta in the sauce and serve with grated Pecorino and a pinch of salt and pepper.

SERVES 6–8

2 medium potatoes
300g spinach leaves, washed
100g salted anchovies or anchovies preserved in oil
3 garlic cloves, peeled
4 tablespoons extra virgin olive oil
200ml cream
500g wholemeal fettuccine or regular fettuccine
50g freshly grated Pecorino
salt and freshly ground black pepper

Anchovy cream is also delicious with spinach and ricotta ravioli. Cook the ravioli in a saucepan of boiling salted water, drain and toss in the anchovy cream.

Sea trout parcels

Trota al cartoccio

Baking fish in parcels ensures delicious, succulent flesh and the presentation of parcels tied up with string adds a nice touch of animation to the table. The parcels can be prepared a couple of hours in advance and placed in the fridge, which is always an advantage when you are cooking for many guests.

Presentation is an important aspect of eating. Italians say, '*Anche l'occhio vuole la sua parte*' – the eye also wants its part. For the festive season you could add a little colourful bow or rosette to your parcels before taking them to the table.

PREHEAT THE OVEN to 200°C. Cut out 12 squares of parchment paper measuring 25cm x 25cm. Cut 12 x 50cm lengths of twine (you could also use fresh chives).

Peel the butternut squash, cut in half lengthways and scrape out the seeds. Cut into tiny cubes.

Heat the olive oil in a large pan over a low heat. Sauté the garlic for about 1 minute, just until it's fragrant but not browned. Remove the garlic with a slotted spoon and discard. Add the butternut squash to the pan and swirl it in the oil. Cover and cook for a couple of minutes. Remove the lid and add the Marsala. Increase the heat momentarily to cook off the alcohol, then reduce the heat again, cover and cook for another 5 minutes, until the squash is tender.

SERVES 12

2 small butternut squash
4 tablespoons extra virgin olive oil, plus extra for drizzling
2 garlic cloves, peeled and left whole
20ml Marsala
120g flaked almonds
12 x 200g fresh sea trout fillets
large sprig of fresh thyme
salt and freshly ground black pepper
butter

Toast the almonds for 30 seconds in a hot, dry pan.

Rub a little oil on the 12 squares of parchment paper. Place a fillet of fish in the middle of each piece of parchment. Sprinkle over some butternut squash and a few thyme leaves. Scatter over some toasted almonds and a pinch of salt and pepper. Drizzle a little olive oil over everything, then place a knob of butter on top of each fish fillet. Bring the paper together in the middle to form a little bundle and seal up the ends to completely enclose the fish. Tie with the twine.

Place the parcels on two baking trays and cook in the oven for 10 minutes. Divide the parcels onto two large serving dishes and bring them to the table. Make sure you have set the table with sharp knives so your guests can either cut open the parcel or simply undo the twine.

You could also use sea bream, sea bass, fresh salmon or hake. Play around with dressings too, such as a citrus dressing or a Mediterranean dressing of olives, tomatoes and capers.

Hake with hazelnut and sage crust

Nasello con crosta di nocciole e salvia

Tonda gentile delle Langhe (gentle round of the Langhe) – what a lovely name for the nicest hazelnuts I have ever eaten. Fragrant and sweet with no bitter aftertaste, they are a choice ingredient for the sumptuous *gianduiotti* chocolates of Turin.

PREHEAT THE OVEN to 200°C.

Put the hazelnuts on a baking tray and toast in the oven for 10–15 minutes, until the skins start to loosen. Remove the skins by piling the nuts onto a clean tea towel, folding over the towel to enclose the nuts and rubbing the nuts until the skins flake away.

Using a pestle and mortar, lightly crush the hazelnuts. Blend the crushed hazelnuts, sage leaves, 4 tablespoons of olive oil and some salt and pepper. Coat one side of each hake fillet with this paste.

Pour the remaining 4 tablespoons of olive oil in a roasting tin. Place the fish in the tin, coated side up, and cook in the oven for about 15 minutes, until the fish is firm to the touch and cooked through. Serve with lemon wedges.

SERVES 6

200g hazelnuts
bunch of fresh sage
8 tablespoons extra virgin olive oil
salt and freshly ground black
    pepper
6 x 150–200g hake fillets, skinned
6 lemon wedges

Speckled sprouts and leeks

Cavoletti di bruxelles con porri e speck

Brussels sprouts are not popular in Italy, but they are my addition to a festive Italian dinner. Stefano's family learned to love and expect them and they became part of the Crescenzis' traditional fare. Nonna Valentina would ask Stefano, '*Ma Cosa porta i cavoletti di bruxelles* (Is Which bringing the sprouts)?' She couldn't pronounce my name and fondly referred to me as *Cosa*, or Which, or as we say in Dublin, 'what's her name'.

COOK THE SPROUTS in boiling salted water for 10 minutes and drain. When they're cool enough to handle, cut the sprouts in half.

Heat the olive oil in a wide, heavy-based pan over a low heat. Sauté the leeks in olive oil for about 5 minutes, until they soften. Add the speck and cook until the colour deepens. Add the sprouts, stir and cook for 2 minutes more. Season with salt and pepper and serve straightaway.

SERVES 6

500g Brussels sprouts
4 tablespoons extra virgin olive oil
4 leeks, finely sliced
200g speck or pancetta, thinly sliced
    and cut into strips
salt and freshly ground black
    pepper

Another version of this dish is to boil the sprouts, drain and whizz in a blender with 200ml fresh cream and 20g freshly grated parmigiano. Serve with a crunchy fried speck topping.

Carrots with parmigiano cream

Carote alla crema di parmigiano

When you invite your Italian friends to dinner, it's expected that children will be included. When we moved to Ireland our children were so disappointed not to be invited along, although I do see the merits of a night off! Children will eat tons of carrots when they're coated in a parmigiano cream.

COOK THE CARROTS in boiling salted water for 5 minutes and drain.

Melt the butter in a large pan and whisk in the parmigiano. Add the carrots and coat with the parmigiano cream.

SERVES 4

500g carrots, peeled and cut into
    1cm x 4cm batons
50g butter
50g freshly grated parmigiano

When there are no children in the party, you can add plenty of freshly ground black pepper.

Christmas cake

Pandolce

Pandolce (sweet bread) is a homely alternative to the traditional shop-bought *panettone* cake. I have adjusted the recipe a little to make it more orange, sweet and, dare I say it, delicious.

PREHEAT THE OVEN to 175℃. Grease a 23cm springform baking tin.

Cream the butter and sugar until it's light and fluffy. Add the eggs one at a time, mixing well to incorporate them each time. Mix in the orange and lemon juice and zest, then stir in the flour and baking powder. Add the raisins and sultanas, candied fruit, nuts, cinnamon and nutmeg. Mix well to a creamy consistency. Pour the batter into the greased baking tin.

Bake in the oven for 1 hour, until a skewer inserted in the centre comes out clean. Leave to rest for 10 minutes before releasing the cake from the tin. Leave to cool on a wire rack.

To make the glaze, place the sugar, orange zest and juice in a small saucepan. Bring up to a simmer and cook for 10 minutes over a low heat, until the sugar has dissolved and the syrup has thickened. Pour over the cake.

SERVES 12

250g butter, softened
250g caster sugar
2 free-range or organic eggs, beaten
zest and juice of 1 orange
zest and juice of 1 lemon
500g self-raising flour
1 level teaspoon baking powder
400g mix of sultanas and raisins
25g candied fruit
25g pine nuts
25g roughly crushed hazelnuts, walnuts or pistachios
2 level teaspoons ground cinnamon
1 level teaspoon grated nutmeg

For the glaze:
200g caster sugar
zest and juice of 2 oranges

Incorporating good-quality chocolate drops adds a touch of decadence.

CHRISTMAS DAY

Il Giorno di Natale

PRESENT

Family and friends

....

ANTIPASTO

Crostini with chicken liver pâté

PASTA

Casarecce pasta with sausage and cream of asparagus

MEAT

Vitello tonnato

Fillet of pork with speck cloak and applesauce

SIDE

Pan-fried spinach with parmigiano and toasted almonds

DESSERT

Toasted *pandoro* ricotta mess

IT TOOK a long time for Santa Claus, fairy lights, Christmas trees

and trinkets to arrive in Italy. Ousting the reigning *Befana* was a long and tedious task. The *Befana* is a scary-looking witch who rides on a broomstick. According to tradition she brings toys and stockings stuffed with sweets to well-behaved children and lumps of coal (or sweets that look like coal) to children who have not been so well behaved on the eve of the sixth of January, or Epiphany. My children loved those sweet nuggets of coal and still ask for them now, as young adults. Nowadays Italians have adopted the Christmas tree and all the other embellishments, but Santa still remains an odd-looking statue in the hall and the cunning *Befana* continues to reign, weaving in and out on her broomstick, disseminating toys and treats.

Christmas in the Crescenzi household has never consisted of anything fewer than 25 guests and we continue this tradition here in Ireland. My children can't imagine a Christmas with only a handful of guests. They tend to invite all and sundry, which is what makes Christmas dinner so special. It's the guests and their stories, habits and cultures that enrich, enliven and enhance each dinner, year in and year out.

Crostini with chicken liver pâté

Crostini Toscani

Crostini Toscani with chicken liver pâté is a warm and hearty starter. I suggest you serve your guests these tasty crostini, along with a very good glass of Chianti Classico, in front of a blazing log fire. Following some effusive conversation, move everyone to the dining table.

CHOP THE LIVERS to a minced consistency (a mezzaluna is good for this).

Heat the olive oil in a large pan over a medium heat. Sauté the shallots for 5 minutes, until they are soft and translucent. Add the anchovies, if using, and mash them with a wooden spoon until they dissolve into the oil. Add the bay leaves and capers, if using, followed by the minced chicken livers. Stir and heat through until the meat takes on a deep pink colour. Pour in the vin santo and increase the heat momentarily to cook off the alcohol. Return to a medium heat, cover and cook for 10 minutes. Season with salt and pepper to taste.

Remove the bay leaves, then remove the pan from the heat and leave to rest.

Cut the bread into 12 slices and toast it lightly.

Spread some pâté on each slice of bread or place in small ramekins to let your guests serve themselves. Place on a serving dish and drizzle with a little oil.

MAKES 12

500g free-range or organic chicken livers

4 tablespoons extra virgin olive oil, plus extra for drizzling

2 shallots, finely sliced

4 anchovies (optional) – I use the salted ones in jars

2 bay leaves

1 tablespoon capers (optional)

100ml vin santo (Tuscan dessert wine)

salt and freshly ground black pepper

2 baguettes or ciabatta loaves

I like the rough consistency of this pâté. If you prefer a smoother pâté, blend it to the consistency you like.

Casarecce pasta with sausage and cream of asparagus

Casarecce con salsicce e crema di asparagi

Casa means home and *casarecce* denotes homemade. These little twists of pasta were very common in rural areas and are relatively easy to make. Whenever I stroll the streets of Italian villages or cities, I can't resist entering shops with the word *casalinghi* invitingly displayed over the doorway. These are tiny homeware shops, mere corridors bursting with displays of dishes, pots and pans of every description, jars, corks, crockery, cookie cutters, knives, measures, oil dispensers, boards and hoards of rarely used gadgets – a gourmand's paradise of mumble jumble.

SQUEEZE THE SAUSAGEMEAT out of its skin.

Bend the asparagus until it naturally snaps and discard the woody ends. Cut the asparagus in half.

Heat 2 tablespoons of the olive oil in a medium saucepan over a medium heat. Sauté the shallot for 5 minutes, until it becomes soft and translucent. Add the asparagus and coat it in the oil, then add the hot water and a pinch of salt. Cover and cook for 5 minutes, then blitz with a hand blender. Stir in the cream.

Cook the pasta in a large saucepan of boiling salted water until al dente or according to the packet instructions.

In a separate large pan, heat the remaining 1 tablespoon of olive oil over a medium heat. Fry the sausagemeat for 3 minutes. Add the creamed asparagus and give it a swirl.

Drain the pasta and place it in a large serving bowl. Mix through the sausage and asparagus cream. Sprinkle generously with freshly grated parmigiano and Pecorino. Serve immediately.

SERVES 6–8

250g fresh Italian salsiccia sausage
500g asparagus
3 tablespoons extra virgin olive oil
1 shallot, finely chopped
250ml hot water
salt
200ml fresh cream
500g casarecce pasta
25g freshly grated parmigiano
25g freshly grated Pecorino

You could use pancetta or guanciale instead of sausage, or omit the pork altogether for your vegetarian guests.

Vitello tonnato

Vitello tonnato is one of those endearing, old-fashioned dishes that everyone adores yet rarely prepares. It's the Italian cousin of prawn cocktail, I suppose.

PREHEAT THE OVEN to 200°C.

Place the veal in a roasting tin and roast for 20 minutes. Leave to cool. Using an electric knife or your sharpest knife, slice the cold veal wafer thin. Lay the slices on a serving plate.

Using a blender, whizz together the tuna, mayonnaise, half the capers, the anchovies and the oil and pour over the veal. Sprinkle over the rest of the capers and the pomegranate seeds, if using. Serve with toasted ciabatta or breadsticks.

SERVES 6

600g fillet of veal (in one piece)
300g yellowfin tuna preserved in oil
150g mayonnaise
20 capers, rinsed
4 salted anchovies, chopped
2 tablespoons extra virgin olive oil
4 tablespoons pomegranate seeds (optional)
toasted ciabatta or breadsticks, to serve

Fillet of pork with speck cloak and applesauce

Filetto di maiale con scialle di speck e salsa di mele cotte

Maurizio, my aunt's husband, spends a great deal of time at his ancestral home perched among the beloved apple orchards of his Val di Non. After every visit, he arrives back with a bottle of pure apple juice.

There was always great excitement when Sheila and Maurizio came to Ireland for a visit. Maurizio would be hauled off to Moroney's pub in Pearse Street for Guinness and chasers of Jameson whiskey. He looked totally out of place, dressed in his perfectly pressed thick corduroy navy trousers, sky blue cashmere sweater, crisp button-down collared shirt, polished proper leather shoes and a splendid charcoal grey cashmere wool coat. One particular evening he returned around midnight to a feast of boiled trotters, ribs and tails – a far cry from his usual *cotechino* – and minus his coat. My father, known locally as Fred the Red, put his arm reassuringly around Maurizio's shoulders. 'Don't worry, my auld flower, it'll turn up and I'll post it over to you.'

The following day, I noted Jack Madden looking particularly smug. Jack was our local homeless person who spent his days chasing cigarette butts from passers-by and travellers disembarking from the No. 3 bus. He was fed by all and accepted as part of our community. And there was Maurizio's coat, embracing Jack like a lord of the manor. Shocked, I waited at the top of our square, ready to intercept my father on his return from work. He soon arrived on his bicycle, in his heavy donkey jacket and oiled overalls, whistling and calling out to all who passed his way. 'What's up, Allanagh?' he said.

Continued overleaf

SERVES 6

6 x 180g chunks of pork fillet
4 tablespoons wholegrain honey mustard
150g smoked speck, thinly sliced
4 tablespoons extra virgin olive oil

For the applesauce:
4 eating apples, such as Melinda or Pink Lady
100ml water
1 tablespoon muscovado sugar or caster sugar

'Jack is wearing Maurizio's coat,' I reported.

'Don't worry. Sure, Maurizio can afford lots more coats, and isn't Jack as snug as a bug?' he retorted with a glint in his eyes. 'Run home and tell your mother to prepare my tea. I'm just going for a quick pint.' Of course, there was never such a thing as a quick pint. I'm not sure if I ever told Maurizio what actually happened to his splendid coat.

TO MAKE THE APPLESAUCE, peel, core and chop the apples. Put the water and sugar in a saucepan and simmer until the sugar dissolves, then add the apples, cover and cook for 15 minutes, until the apples have softened. Blend to a smooth consistency.

Pound the pieces of pork until they are all about 5cm thick. Coat lightly with the mustard. Wrap each chunk of pork in speck and secure with a toothpick.

Heat the oil in a wide, heavy-based saucepan over a medium heat. Add the pork and seal on all sides. Cover and cook for 6 minutes on each side. Serve with a helping of applesauce.

You could use pancetta or guanciale instead of speck. Sometimes I like to add raisins and pine nuts to the applesauce if the fancy takes me.

Pan-fried spinach with parmigiano and toasted almonds

Spinaci al burro, parmigiano e mandorle tostate

During my stays in Rome I like to buy kilos of fresh spinach from the fruit and vegetable market in Piazza San Cosimato in Trastevere. The dark green purplish leaves are laden down with thick organic muck and beautiful red stems sprout out here and there. I wash the spinach five times in a big basin of cold water or until the water remains clear, then nimbly cut away those beautiful stems and immerse the leaves in boiling salted water. The taste of those big misshapen leaves is extraordinary, quite unlike the pre-washed mellow spinach that most of us are used to today. I can still remember the muck on my hands and the wonderful taste and smell of that organic spinach, but it is difficult to recall any such affiliation with cultivated spinach.

COOK THE SPINACH in a large saucepan of boiling salted water for 1 minute and drain very well (organic spinach may take a little longer).

Toast the almonds for 30 seconds on a hot, dry pan.

Melt the butter in a wide, heavy-based saucepan. Add the parmigiano and whisk to combine. Add the spinach to the saucepan and mix through. Remove from the heat.

Serve with a sprinkle of toasted almonds and season with salt and freshly ground black pepper.

SERVES 6–8

1kg spinach leaves, washed (or 2kg organic spinach, washed as outlined in the introduction)
20g flaked almonds
20g butter
100g freshly grated parmigiano
salt and freshly ground black pepper

On hot summer days I prefer to eat spinach cold, dressed with good extra virgin olive oil and lemon juice.

Toasted *pandoro* ricotta mess

Pasticcio di ricotta con pandoro tostato

Pandoro from Verona is the sister of *panettone*, a light vanilla sponge with a delicate sugary coating. Just as the Magi took gold, frankincense and myrrh to Bethlehem, beautifully packaged *pandoro*, *panettone*, *torrone*, *panforte* and other regional sweets are brought as offerings from home to home throughout Italy during the festive season.

MELT THE BUTTER in a wide, heavy-based saucepan. Toast the *pandoro* cubes in the melted butter and set aside.

Whip the ricotta in a large mixing bowl (or for 30 seconds if using an electric mixer) and fold in the sugar, chocolate, candied orange peel, cinnamon and toasted *pandoro*.

Place a couple of raspberries at the bottom of six individual glasses. Spoon the ricotta mess on top and sprinkle with the crushed pistachios.

Serve immediately or cover with cling film and refrigerate for up to two days.

SERVES 6

50g butter

2 thick slices of *pandoro*, cut into small cubes (about 200g)

250g fresh ricotta

50g caster sugar

50g 70% dark chocolate, grated

40g candied orange peel (page 62), finely diced (optional)

¼ teaspoon ground cinnamon

125g fresh raspberries

30g shelled pistachio nuts, crushed

ST STEPHEN'S DAY (BOXING DAY)

Il Giorno di Santo Stefano

PRESENT

Family, relatives and stragglers

....

ANTIPASTO

Salumi antipasto with chilli salami muffins and chilli and prune compote

PASTA

Lasagna with porcini mushrooms, speck and saffron

Gnocchetti sardi with saffron, courgettes and Pecorino

MAINS

Beef or veal skewers with mortadella and sage

SIDES

Pan-fried courgettes with mint and vinegar

DESSERT

Panettone with orange custard and raspberry coulis

ONE YEAR, my friends Imelda and Loretta, two charming,

glamorous ladies and renowned Irish art gallerists, suggested we take a trip to Florence on St Stephen's Day to take in the Uffizi galleries, do a spot of shopping and dine at one of Florence's sophisticated eateries. We headed for the Stazione Termini (Rome's central train station), all dolled up for a day in the Renaissance city of Florence, and took our seats in the first-class compartment, as ladies of such social standing would do. The train took off and soon the ticket controller passed by. '*Ma lei, dove pensa che sta andando* (Where do you think you are going)?' he asked quite grumpily. '*Firenze*,' I retorted. He exploded into laughter. '*Ma lei sta andando a Napoli* (You are going to Naples)!' He continued along the corridor, relating our misadventure to all on board, and we became the topic of conversation for the entire compartment for the duration of the journey.

With undue prejudice I instructed the ladies to remove their jewellery, pushed my own earrings, bracelets and credit cards down my boots and drilled them on how to survive a day in Napoli. It's the home of the Gomorrah, after all. After a short one-hour train journey we emerged into the warmth of the bustling Neapolitan metropolis. Determined to make good on the day, I hailed a cab and asked the driver to take us on a tour of Naples. Our taxi driver turned out to be more qualified and *simpatico* than any tour guide. He not only took us to all the usual historical tourist attractions, but offered us the best cappuccino ever at his local coffee bar overlooking the Bay of Naples, brought us to the pastry shop with the most scrumptious *sfogliatelle* pastries stuffed with fresh ricotta and candied fruits and suggested we buy our husbands handmade silk ties from a tiny but beautiful shop, Marinella. He instructed the ancient shopkeeper to treat us well – we had become his new best friends. Our farewell consisted of numerous hugs and *arrivedercis* and he left us to savour a delicious pizza at Napoli Sparita, washed down with some local Greco di Tufo. At one point the young owner overheard us admiring a tempting display of rum baba (sponge cake soaked in rum) in a shop window across the way. He didn't hesitate to pop over, grab a couple and serve them to us along with a ton of admiration for his neighbour in the pastry shop. The pizza was the best we had ever eaten, the wine was even better and the rum baba was unsurpassable.

We stepped out into a marvellous and unexpected spectacle: a procession of colour entwining the tiny streets. The alleyways surrounding Via San Gregorio Armeno were lined with thousands of beautifully crafted *presepi* (cribs). Handmade terracotta figurines dressed in medieval and baroque clothing – some tiny, some life size, including figures dressed as carpenters, bakers, ironmongers, shepherds, *pizzaiole*, lords and ladies – offered a mesmerising display. This is Italy – a surprise around every corner. It turned out to be *un giorno indimenticabile* (an unforgettable day).

Salumi antipasto with chilli salami muffins and chilli and prune compote

Antipasto di salumi con muffin salato e salsa piccante alle prugne

A really good antipasto of salumi comes down to sourcing good-quality charcuterie, having a good variety and assembling it aesthetically. Try eating a thick slice of freshly cut salami compared to a wafer-thin slice of plastic packaged salami and there is no turning back. If you live near a good deli, source some good freshly cut hams and salami and eat within a couple of days. My favourite shops in Italy are Falorni in Greve in Tuscany, Norcineria, Campo di Fiore in Rome and Funari at Servigliano in the Marche. It's worth going out of your way to visit these places and to stock up. Liven up your antipasti with some savoury muffins and a prune compote.

ROLL OR FOLD THE SALUMI slices and arrange decoratively on a large board or plate. Scatter the olives, sun-dried tomatoes and figs on top. Serve with the chilli salami muffins (page 310) and chilli and prune compote (page 311).

SERVES 6

6 slices of Parma ham
6 slices of Milano salami
6 slices of speck
6 slices of lonza
6 slices of Calabrian chilli salame
6 slices of Tuscan wild boar salame
3 slices of mortadella, halved
500g stoned Italian black olives
12 sun-dried tomatoes or fresh, ripe cherry tomatoes on the vine
6 fresh figs, halved

I have suggested various types of cold cuts, but you can choose your favourites. If you decide against making the muffins, make sure you serve your antipasti with chunky bread or focaccia.

Chilli salami muffins

Muffin piccante

These chilli muffins add an interesting touch to your antipasto plates. Use colourful, festive paper cases and serve on a tiered cake stand with small ramekins or mini muffin cases filled with prune and chilli compote.

PREHEAT THE OVEN to 180°C. Line a muffin tin with festive paper cases.

Cream the butter and sugar together until light and fluffy. Add the eggs one at a time, mixing well to incorporate.

Add in the flour, chopped salami and a pinch of salt. Mix until just combined.

Fill each case halfway with the batter. Bake in the oven for 20 minutes, until the muffins are golden brown and a skewer inserted into the centre comes out clean. Turn the muffins out of the tin and transfer to a wire rack to cool.

MAKES 12

100g butter, softened
50g granulated sugar
2 free-range or organic eggs
200g self-raising flour, sifted
100g chilli salami slices, chopped
pinch of salt

Chilli and prune compote

Salsa piccante alle prugne

Soak the prunes in water for 1 hour. Drain the water and remove the stones from the prunes.

Melt the butter in a saucepan over a low heat. Sweat the onion for about 5 minutes, until softened, then stir in the prosciutto and chilli flakes. Pour in the vinegar and increase the heat until all the vinegar has evaporated. Add the prunes, warm water, bay leaf and a pinch of salt. Cover and cook for 45 minutes, until the compote is thick and jammy. Remove the bay leaf and leave to rest for 1 hour or so for the flavours to marry together.

Makes 200ml

250g dried prunes
50g butter
1 small onion, finely sliced
30g prosciutto, roughly chopped into small pieces (optional)
1 teaspoon dried chilli flakes or 1 fresh red chilli, deseeded and finely chopped
125ml balsamic vinegar
125ml warm water
1 bay leaf
pinch of salt

Lasagna with porcini mushrooms, speck and saffron

Lasagna con funghi porcini, speck e zafferano

We celebrate Stefano's *onomastico* (name day) on Santo Stefano, St Stephen's Day. Lasagna with porcini mushrooms has become our family favourite and is anticipated each year by our children (and the 20 other guests, needless to say). Creating family favourites adds a sense of expectation and suspense to festive dinners and cultivates warm family memories. Children love traditional celebrations and enjoy the foods involved.

Stefano's parents celebrated his name day when he was growing up, and once we were married, that task was handed over to us. A grand number of relatives were invited to ours and from early morning he would receive numerous phone calls from distant relatives, all ringing to say, '*Auguri per l'onomastico, Stefano* (Best wishes on your name day).' We transported this tradition to Ireland, and now my family, all authentic Dubliners, expect a slap-up meal on Stefano's name day.

My brothers enjoy taunting Stefano. 'It's the Don's name day,' they say, 'bring out the wine!' Stefano, ever the proud Roman, instantly puts them in their places: 'Which wine would you like? That New World peach juice you are used to? Or would you like to try Elio Grasso's Langhe Chardonnay?' 'Bring on the Grassi, Stef,' they retort, winking and nudging each other. It's Roman sarcasm versus Dublin wit. Our children, nieces and nephews love the banter that threads through the evening.

SOAK THE MUSHROOMS in the milk and hot water and leave for 2 hours.

To make the béchamel, melt the butter in a heavy-based saucepan. When it's foaming, add in the flour little by little,

SERVES 8–12

200g dried porcini mushrooms
250ml milk
50ml hot water
4 tablespoons extra virgin olive oil, plus extra for greasing
knob of butter
2 shallots, diced
200g cured speck, thinly sliced into 2cm x 1cm pieces
100ml dry white wine
1 level teaspoon salt
250ml fresh cream
300g dried lasagne sheets or 600g fresh lasagna sheets
200g freshly grated parmigiano

For the béchamel sauce:
50g butter
50g plain flour
500ml milk
2 sachets of saffron

stirring continuously until it has all been absorbed. Gradually pour in the milk, whisking continuously until all of the milk has been incorporated. Dissolve the saffron in a little milk and add to the pot. Continue to stir over a low heat until the sauce thickens and coats the back of a spoon. Remove from the heat, cover the sauce directly with cling film to prevent a skin from forming and set aside.

Preheat the oven to 200℃.

Heat the olive oil and a knob of butter in a wide, heavy-based saucepan over a low heat. Sweat the shallots for about 5 minutes, until they are soft and translucent.

In a separate hot, dry pan, fry the speck until it's crisp. Set aside.

Strain the milk that the mushrooms have been soaking in and set it aside. Add the mushrooms to the pan with the shallots. Pour in the wine and increase the heat momentarily to cook off the alcohol. Return to a low heat and add the salt. Pour in the strained milk and the cream, heat through and set aside.

Paint a little oil onto the base of a rectangular or square oven dish (mine is 22cm x 27cm). Line the bottom with lasagne sheets. Spoon over a thin layer of porcini sauce, then drizzle with the saffron béchamel. Dot with speck and a generous sprinkling of parmigiano. Repeat the process for another three layers, finishing with a sprinkling of parmigiano.

Cook in the oven for about 30 minutes, until the top is golden and bubbling and you can cut through the lasagne easily. Let the lasagne stand for 10 minutes before cutting.

Gnocchetti sardi with saffron, courgettes and Pecorino

Gnocchetti sardi con zafferano, zucchine e pecorino

Saturday evenings were spent at the Fiddler's Elbow pub sheltered in a side street of San Giovanni. Here a number of girls met their partners, flirting to the tunes of the Róisín Dubh. Propelled by a secret amore for our dear friend Helen, Claudio, a stalwart Sardinian, organised a trip to his *terra*. Upon embarking on the boat at Civitavecchia, the guys were surprised at our lack of luggage. '*La tenda*? Where is the tent? Where are your sleeping bags?' Camping and the requisite paraphernalia was quite alien to us given our inclement Irish weather. 'Oh Claudio, when are we going to eat these wonderful gnocchetti sardi you keep tantalising us with?' I asked, quickly changing the subject. 'They are called malloreddus locally, with yellow saffron like the Sardinian sand and green courgettes like our hillsides. I know the best place for us all to have dinner tonight.'

Serves 6

500g dried gnocchetti sardi pasta
4 tablespoons extra virgin olive oil
1 medium onion, diced small
3 medium courgettes, diced small
1 sachet of saffron
salt and freshly ground black pepper
25g grated Pecorino Romano

COOK THE PASTA in a large saucepan of boiling salted water until al dente or according to the packet instructions.

Heat the olive oil in a large, wide saucepan over a low heat. Sauté the onion for 5 minutes until it is starting to soften and turn translucent. Add the courgettes, cover the pan and cook for 5 minutes, stirring occasionally.

Dissolve the saffron in half a ladle of water taken from the pasta pot. Add the saffron liquid and some salt and pepper to the pan with the onions and courgettes. Stir and cook for another 5 minutes, then remove from the heat.

Drain the pasta and place it in a large serving bowl. Pour over the saffron courgettes and sprinkle with a generous helping of grated Pecorino. Serve immediately.

Beef or veal skewers with mortadella and sage

Involtini con mortadella e salvia

Involtini are thin slivers of meat, fish or vegetables rolled around cheese, vegetables, herbs, fruit or salumi, either cooked or served raw. The combinations are infinite. Sicilians tend to use a lot of stale bread in their cooking, which is a clever way of utilising every crumb. Mind you, we are talking about good bread: sourdough or a good crusty loaf. The bread absorbs the juices of the pancetta and becomes a succulent bite.

PREHEAT THE OVEN to 200°C. Grease a baking tray with some olive oil.

Wrap each chunk of bread in a slice of pancetta.

Loosely wrap each slice of meat in cling film and pound until it's wafer thin. Remove the cling film and place a piece of mortadella and a sage leaf on each slice. Roll up loosely and insert a metal skewer through two rolls with a wedge of red onion in between.

Place a pancetta-wrapped bread chunk at the beginning and end of the skewer. Prepare six skewers in this way.

Place the skewers on the oiled baking tray. Place the tray in the oven and roast for 15 minutes, turning the skewers throughout the cooking time, until the meat is nicely browned and the onions have charred a little.

SERVES 6

extra virgin olive oil

12 chunks of stale bread, cut into 3cm squares

6 thin slices of pancetta, each slice cut in half

12 x 60g pieces of thinly sliced topside of beef or veal

4 slices of mortadella, cut into 12 pieces

12 fresh sage leaves

3 medium red onions, peeled and quartered

I have also used pannetone in this recipe, which works nicely too.

Pan-fried courgettes with mint and vinegar

Zucchine saltate in padella con aceto e menta

A light side dish of courgettes is a fitting companion for a heavy meal.

TRIM THE ENDS OFF THE COURGETTES and cut the courgettes into 1cm-thick circles.

Heat the oil in a wide saucepan over a low heat. Sauté the garlic and mint leaves for about 1 minute, just until the garlic is fragrant but not browned. Add the vinegar and increase the heat momentarily to let some of it evaporate. Add the courgettes, cover and cook for 10 minutes, stirring regularly. Season with salt to taste.

SERVES 8–10

800g medium courgettes
6 tablespoons extra virgin olive oil
2 garlic cloves, thinly sliced
6 fresh mint leaves
3 tablespoons white wine vinegar
salt

Pan-fried courgettes are delicious as a bruschetta topping. Serve on toasted ciabatta and garnish with a mint leaf.

Panettone with orange custard and raspberry coulis

Panettone con crema all'arancia e succo di lampone

If you still have some *panettone* hanging around, jostling with the carafes and candelabra on top of the sideboard, here is a delicious way to serve this traditional cake.

To make the custard, put the milk, cream and orange zest in a heavy-based saucepan and bring to a simmer.

In a separate large bowl, whisk together the egg yolks, sugar and cornflour really well, until thick and pale. Whisk a little of the warm milk into the egg yolk mixture, then slowly pour in the rest of the milk, whisking continuously so the eggs don't scramble. Slice the vanilla pod lengthways and scrape the seeds into the bowl.

Pour the custard back into the saucepan and cook gently over a low heat for a couple of minutes, stirring with a wooden spoon until the custard thickens and coats the back of the spoon.

To make the coulis, quickly blend all the ingredients together. Pass through a fine-mesh sieve into a jug or bowl, cover with cling film and refrigerate.

Lay the *panettone* on its side and cut into eight to 12 circular slices 2cm thick (how many slices you can get out of your cake depends on how big it is). Sandwich four slices together with a generous dollop of the orange custard between each slice as well as a layer of custard on top. Dust with icing sugar and serve with a drizzle of raspberry coulis.

Serves 8–12

1 x 500g *panettone*
icing sugar, for dusting

For the orange custard:
550ml fresh milk
50ml fresh cream
zest of 2 oranges
4 organic or free-range egg yolks
50g caster sugar
2 level teaspoons cornflour
1 vanilla pod

For the raspberry coulis:
200g fresh raspberries
50g caster sugar
zest of ½ lemon

INDEX

Aeolian islands, 217

al dente, 16

Alba, 240

All Saints and All Souls Days, 247–9
    Caprese flourless chocolate cake, 260
    dumplings in capon broth, 250, 252
    pan-fried butternut squash and oregano, 257
    pappardelle with braised wild boar stracotto, 253
    rabbit and chicken casserole, 225–6
    ricotta and cherry tart, 258–9

allegria salad, 73

Altamura crostini, 53

Amarena cherries, 258–9

amatriciana, 15

anchovy cream, 281

Antonelli, Filippo, 84

applesauce, 299–300

apricot and basil compote, 202

Arborio rice, 17, 117, 154–5, 200–1, 232–3

arrabbiata sauces, 14, 46–7, 50, 54

artichoke
    artichoke and lamb coratella, 132
    Romanesco, 34, 36

Asiago cheese, 70, 205, 268

asparagus
    cream of, 296
    risotto with scallops and saffron, 183
    risotto with smoked salmon and lemon, 102–3
    warm asparagus salad, 204–5

aubergine
    aubergine parmigiana, 105
    caponata vegetable antipasto, 198–9

bagna cauda, 98

baked crostini with mozzarella, prosciutto and figs, 48

balsamic and garlic French beans, 123

balsamic reduction, 114

Barbera wine, 117, 119, 227

basil, 16

beaches, 210–11

béchamel sauce, 16, 134–5, 312–13

beef
    beef skewers with mortadella and sage, 316
    porcini meatloaf with truffle oil and tomato
      sauce, 69
    tagliata with truffle, 244

bella ciao anthem, 162–3

birthday and names day dinner, 195–7
    caponata vegetable antipasto, 198–9
    meatballs with apricot and basil compote, 202
    risotto with mushrooms and duck with thyme,
      200–1
    tiramisù with vin santo, 207
    warm asparagus salad, 204–5

biscuits
    Cantuccini biscuits with cranberries and
      chocolate, 28
    Ciambellini wine biscuits, 57
    ladyfinger, 207

boar stracotto, 253

bottarga tonnarelli, 149

Boxing Day *see* St Stephen's Day

bresaola, robiola and honey rolls, 182

broad bean and Pecorino salad, 164

broccoli
    and anchovies, 156
    broccoli rabe, 99–100
    crespelle with smoked mozzarella and broccoli,
      134–5
    fettucine with broccoli, orange, anchovies and
      Pecorino, 215

bruschetta
    al pomodoro, 17
    with burrata, wilted radicchio, toasted pine nuts
      and balsamic reduction, 114
    garlic, 18

Brussel sprouts, 286
burrata, 114
butternut squash, pan-fried, 257

cakes
    lemon ciambella with pistachio glaze, 172–3,
      175
    limoncello rice pudding, 42
    mignon cakes, 172, 204
    pastiera, 140–1
Calabrese swordfish pizzaiola, 152
calamari, fried, 236
camomile tea, 130, 131
canapés with smoked salmon, soft goat's cheese,
    rocket and candied orange, 62
cannellini bean, celery, sun-dried tomato and
    avocado salad, 170
Cantuccini biscuits with cranberries and
    chocolate, 28
capon broth, 250, 252
caponata vegetable antipasto, 198–9
Caporale, Tonino, 51
Caprese flourless chocolate cake, 260
caramels, walnut, prune and pancetta, 84
Carnaroli rice, 17, 117, 154–5, 200–1
carnevale, 59–61
    allegria salad, 73
    canapés with smoked salmon, soft goat's
      cheese, rocket and candied orange, 62
    castagnole mini doughnuts, 75
    children's tomato sauce with hidden
      vegetables, 65
    courgette and speck frittata, 68
    frappe, 76
    nutella pizza, 78–9
    pizza margherita with finocchiona salami, 70,
      72
    porcini meatloaf with truffle oil and tomato
      sauce, 69
    spinach, ricotta and pine nut tart, 66–7
    timballo of pasta with tomato, speck and
      aubergine, 63–4
carpaccio, swordfish, 274
carrots with parmigiano cream, 287
casalinghi, 296
casarecce pasta with sausage and cream of
    asparagus, 296
casserole
    polenta gratin, 268

rabbit and chicken, 225–6
sardine, 217
castagnole mini doughnuts, 75
chantarelle mushrooms, 150–1, 243
cheese fritters, 237
cherry and ricotta tart, 258–9
chicken
    chicken and rabbit casserole, 225–6
    chicken liver pâté, 294
    roasted and stuffed, 187–8
chickpea vellutata, 88–9
children's tomato sauce with hidden vegetables, 65
chilli and prune compote, 308, 310, 311
chilli flakes, 15, 51
chilli salami muffins, 308, 310
chips, 190
chocolate cake, Caprese, 260
Christmas cake, 289
Christmas Day, 291, 293
    casarecce pasta with sausage and cream of
      asparagus, 296
    crostini with chicken liver pâté, 294
    fillet of pork with speck cloak and applesauce,
      299–300
    pan-fried spinach with parmigiano and toasted
      almonds, 301
    toasted pandoro ricotta mess, 302
    vitello tonnato, 297
Christmas Eve dinner, 271–3
    carrots with parmigiano cream, 287
    Christmas cake, 289
    fettucine with spinach, potato and anchovy
      sauce, 281
    hake with hazelnut and sage crust, 284
    sea trout parcels, 282–3
    speckled sprouts and leeks, 286
    swordfish carpaccio with capers, 274
    tonnarelli with shellfish, 279–80
    tuna tartare with citrus dressing, 275
Ciambellini wine biscuits, 57
citrus dressing, 275
clams, 85, 180, 279–80
cod with prawn cream sauce, 186
coffee granita, 125
Colonnata lard, 24
compote
    apricot and basil, 202
    chilli and prune, 308, 310, 311
coratella, 132

coulis
    passion fruit, 93
    raspberry, 318
courgette
    caponata vegetable antipasto, 198–9
    chips, 230
    courgette and speck frittata, 68
    flowers, 86, 230
    gnocchetti sardi, 315
    pan-fried with mint and vinegar, 317
    pesto, 85
    stuffed, 120, 122
cream, 17
crêpes, 134–5
crespelle with smoked mozzarella and broccoli,
  134–5
crostini
    Altamura, 53
    baked, with mozzarella, prosciutto and figs, 48
    with chicken liver pâté, 294
    with Colonnata lard, 24
    polenta, with Swiss chard and Gorgonzola, 267
crudités with pinzimonio and bagna cauda, 98
culatello di zibello, 90
custard cream, 107–8
custard fritters, 126–7

dark chocolate Neapolitan pastiera cake, 140–1
della donna, la festa see women's day mimosa
  dinner
dessert wine, 28, 57, 157, 207, 294
dining rooms, 9
doughnuts, Castagnole mini, 75
duck, 200–1
dumplings in capon broth, 250, 252

Easter Sunday and Monday lunch, 129–31
    crespelle with smoked mozzarella and broccoli,
      134–5
    dark chocolate Neapolitan pastiera cake, 140–1
    grilled lamb chops with mint pesto, 137–8
    lamb and artichoke coratella, 132
    roast potatoes, peppers and black olives, 139
eggs and peas, 54
Energe, Giuseppina, 70, 140
Epiphany lunch, 31, 33
    braised Romanesco artichokes, 34, 36
    limoncello rice pudding cake, 42

pennette with mussels, aubergines and ricotta,
  37–8
pork escalopes with a pistachio crust, 39
red cabbage and Teroldego wine, 41
Eucalipto, 134

fairy cakes, 172–3
fare la scarpetti, 180
farfalle pasta salad with cherry tomatoes, tuna,
  pine nuts and mandarins, 166
Father's Day, 111–12
    balsamic and garlic French beans, 123
    bruschetta with burrata, wilted radicchio,
      toasted pine nuts and balsamic reduction, 114
    custard fritters, 126–7
    Giorgio's coffee granita, 125
    risotto with radicchio, pancetta and Barbera,
      117, 119
    schiaffoni with wild hare, 116
    stuffed courgettes, 120, 122
Ferragosto see mid-August holiday lunch
la festa della donna see women's day mimosa
  dinner
fettucine
    with broccoli, orange, anchovies and Pecorino,
      215
    with spinach, potato and anchovy sauce, 281
fig jam, 212, 214
figs, 48
finocchiona salami, 70, 72
Fontina cheese, 146, 205, 237
food stores, 18
foraging, 150
Forno Campo di Fiore, 70
frappe, 76–7
Frascati, 227
French beans, 123
frittata
    courgette and speck, 68
    Tropea red onion, pancetta and potato, 169

garlic and chilli spaghetti, 51
garlic-infused oil, 16
Giorgio's coffee granita, 125
gnocchetti
    with chantarelle mushrooms and sun-dried
      tomatoes, 150–1
    sardi with saffron, courgettes and Pecorino, 315

The Golden Bar, 120
Gorgonzola, 267
granita, 125
green olives, stuffed, 228–9
Grottazzolina, 226–7

hake with hazelnut and sage crust, 284
hare, 116

Il Pompiere, 34
involtini, 316

jam, figs, 212, 214

kiwi, pistachio and feta salad, 106

la festa della donna *see* women's day mimosa
    dinner
Labour Day picnic, 161–3
    bella ciao anthem, 162–3
    cannellini bean, celery, sun-dried tomato and
        avocado salad, 170
    farfalle pasta salad with cherry tomatoes, tuna,
        pine nuts and mandarins, 166
    lemon ciambella with pistachio glaze, 172–3, 175
    pecorino and broad bean salad, 164
    rice salad with tuna and pickles, 167
    Tropea red onion, pancetta and potato frittata,
        169
ladyfinger biscuits, 207
lamb
    grilled chops, 137–8
    lamb and artichoke coratella, 132
lard, Colonnata, 24
lasagna
    porcini mushrooms, speck and saffron, 312–13
    vegetarian, 18
leeks, 286
lemon ciambella with pistachio glaze, 172–3, 175
Lent, 112
lentils
    lentil soup, 24
    New Year's Eve, 23
    and sausages, 27
limoncello rice pudding cake, 42
L'Uliverto, 132

Marcello's bar, 222
mare e monti, 88

Mario, Zio, 54, 150
Marsala dessert wine, 157
Marsala plums with whipped cream, 157, 159
La Mattanza, 275
meatballs, 15, 202
meatloaf, porcini mushrooms with truffle oil and
    tomato sauce, 69
melon, 212, 214
merenda, 172–4
mid-August holiday lunch, 209–11, 214
    fettucine with broccoli, orange, anchovies and
        Pecorino, 215
    Parma ham, melon and fig jam, 212, 214
    peaches in wine, 223
    roast pistacchio quails, 218
    sardine casserole, 217
    tomato peperonata, 221–2
midnight suppers, 45–6
    baked crostini with mozzarella, prosciutto and
        figs, 48
    Ciambellini wine biscuits, 57
    spaghettata of garlic and chilli spaghetti, 51
    tomato and chilli penne, 50
    velvety vegetable soup with Altamura crostini, 53
    Zio Mario's eggs and peas, 54
mignon cakes, 172, 204
mimosa
    mimosa branches, 96, 97
    mimosa cake, 107–8
minced meat, 16
minestrone soup, 53
mini doughnuts, 75
mint pesto, 137–8
mistrà, 191, 193
monkfish with rosemary chickpeas and crispy
    prosciutto, 88–9
Mother's Day, 143, 145
    Calabrese swordfish pizzaiola, 152
    Fontina cheese and ham strudel, 146
    gnocchetti with chantarelle mushrooms and
        sun-dried tomatoes, 150–1
    Marsala plums with whipped cream, 157, 159
    Romanesco broccoli and anchovies, 156
    Sardinian bottarga tonnarelli, 149
    tomatoes stuffed with saffron rice, 154–5
muffins, chilli salami, 308, 310
mushrooms *see* chantarelle mushrooms; porcini
    mushrooms; sauces, sausage and mushroom
mussels, 37–8, 279–80

names day dinner *see* birthday and names day
  dinner
Naples, 22, 140, 141, 306–7
Neapolitan pastiera cake, 140–1
New Year's Eve, 21–3
  Cantuccini biscuits with cranberries and
    chocolate, 28
  lentil soup with Colonnata lardo crostini, 24
  lentils and sausages, 27
nutella pizza, 78–9

October truffle celebrations, 239–40
  pan-fried chantarelle mushrooms with truffle,
    243
  tagliata of beef with truffle, 244
  tagliolini with truffle and anchovies, 242
  tartine with truffle butter, 241
olive oil, 17–18, 157
olive oil and rosemary chips, 190
olives, stuffed, 228–9
orange custard, 318
orecchiette with broccoli rabe, Italian sausage and
  fennel fronds, 99–100
oregano, 257

Pa Piscina, Venice, 106
pancetta, 15, 63–4, 68, 84, 117, 119, 169, 268, 286, 316
pandolce, 289
pandoro ricotta mess, 302
panettone with orange custard and raspberry
  coulis, 318
pannacotta with passion fruit coulis, 93
pappardelle with braised wild boar stracotto, 253
Parma ham, melon and fig jam, 212, 214
parmigiano, 15, 54, 105, 287
Il Pasquino, 222
passion fruit coulis, 93
pasta sauces, 14–15 *see also* sauces
pastarelle, 172
pastiera cakes, 140–1
peaches in wine, 223
Pecorino, 15, 54, 85, 137, 164, 215, 315
penne, tomato and chilli, 50
pennette with mussels, aubergines and ricotta, 37–8
peppers, 198–9, 221–2
pesto, 85, 137–8, 185
pickles, 167
pine nuts, 66–7, 114, 120, 122, 163, 166, 185, 198–9,
  258–9

pinzimonio, 98
pistachio glaze, 172–3, 175
pistachio nuts, 39, 218
pizza
  margherita with finocchiona salami, 70, 72
  nutella, 78–9
  with peaches and mistrà, 191, 193
Pizza Pazza, 154
pizzaiola, swordfish, 152
plums with whipped cream, 157, 159
polenta, 218, 253
  polenta crostini with Swiss chard and
    Gorgonzola, 267
  polenta gratin with speck and Asiago, 268
  with sausages and mushrooms, 266
porcini mushrooms, 18, 69, 132, 150, 312–13
pork
  escalopes with a pistachio crust, 39
  fillet with speck cloak and applesauce, 299–300
  pancetta, 15, 63–4, 68, 84, 117, 119, 169, 268,
    286, 316
potatoes, roasted, 139
prawn cream sauce, 186
prawns, 185
prune and chilli compote, 308, 310, 311

quails, roast pistacchio, 218

rabbit and chicken casserole, 225–6
radicchio, 98, 114, 117, 119, 132, 201
ragù, 15, 16
raspberry coulis, 318
red cabbage and Teroldego wine, 41
religious festivities, 177, 179
  bresaola, robiola and honey rolls, 182
  cod with prawn cream sauce, 186
  olive oil and rosemary chips, 190
  pizza with peaches and mistrà, 191, 193
  risotto with white asparagus, scallops and
    saffron, 183
  roast stuffed chicken, 187–8
  sauté of clams with toast, 180
  trofie with pesto and prawns, 185
resting, 15
rice
  rice pudding cake, 42
  rice salad with tuna and pickles, 167
  saffron rice, 154–5

ricotta
    ricotta and cherry tart, 258–9
    whipped, 37–8
risottos
    cooking, 17
    with courgette flowers, peas and walnuts, 86
    with mushrooms and duck with thyme, 200–1
    with radicchio, pancetta and Barbera wine,
        117, 119
    with smoked salmon, asparagus and lemon,
        102–3
    with white asparagus, scallops and saffron, 183
robiola cheese, 182
Romanesco artichokes, 34, 36
Romanesco broccoli and anchovies, 156
rosticceria, 154

sacred sagre street food *see* sagre street food
saffron rice, 154–5
sagre street food, 225–7
    cheese fritters, 237
    fried calamari, 236
    stuffed courgette flowers, 230
    stuffed green olives, 228–9
    supplì, 232–3
salads
    allegria, 73
    cannellini bean, celery, sun-dried tomato and
        avocado, 170
    farfalle pasta with cherry tomatoes, tuna, pine
        nuts and mandarins, 166
    heirloom tomato, rocket and carpaccio of
        mushroom, 91
    kiwi, pistachio and feta, 106
    Pecorino and broad bean salad, 164
    rice with tuna and pickles, 167
    warm asparagus, 204–5
salami, 70, 72, 187, 308, 310
Salina, 217
salsiccia sausage, 27, 187–8, 266, 296
salumi antipasto, 308
sardine casserole, 217
Sardinian bottarga tonnarelli, 149
sauces
    arrabbiata, 14, 46–7, 50, 54
    children's tomato sauce with hidden
        vegetables, 65
    meatballs with apricot and basil compote, 202
    pasta, 14–15

prawn cream, 186
sausage and mushroom, 266
sauté of clams, 180
spinach, potato and anchovy, 281
tomato, 14, 65, 69, 105, 120, 232–3
scallops, 183
schiaffoni with wild hare, 116
sea trout parcels, 282–3
settembrini, 48
shellfish, 279–80
Shire, Lidia, 37
ski supper, 263–5
    polenta crostini with Swiss chard and
        Gorgonzola, 267
    polenta gratin with speck and Asiago, 268
    polenta with sausages and mushrooms, 266
smoked salmon, 62, 102–3
soffritto, 14, 149, 228, 253
soups
    lentil soup with Colonnata lardo crostini, 24
    minestrone, 53
spaghetti dishes
    Sardinian bottarga tonnarelli, 149
    spaghettata of garlic and chilli spaghetti, 51
    spaghetti with clams and courgette pesto, 85
speck, 63–4, 68, 268, 286, 299–300
spinach
    pan-fried with parmigiano and toasted
        almonds, 301
    spinach, potato and anchovy sauce, 281
    spinach, ricotta and pine nut tart, 66–7
sponge cake, 15, 107–8
squid, fried, 236
St Stephen's Day, 305–7
    beef or veal skewers with mortadella and sage,
        316
    chilli and prune compote, 311
    chilli salami muffins, 310
    gnocchetti sardi with saffron, courgettes and
        Pecorino, 315
    lasagna with porcini mushrooms, speck and
        saffron, 312–13
    panettone with orange custard and raspberry
        coulis, 318
    pan-fried courgettes with mint and vinegar,
        317
    salumi antipasto with chilli salami muffins and
        chilli and prune compote, 308

St Valentine's Day, 81
    heirloom tomato, rocket and carpaccio of
        mushroom salad, 91
    monkfish with rosemary chickpeas and crispy
        prosciutto, 88–9
    risotto with courgette flowers, peas and
        walnuts, 86
    spaghetti with clams and courgette pesto, 85
    veal straccetti with sage and culatello di
        zibello, 90
    walnut, prune and pancetta caramels, 84
stracotto, 15, 253
Stromboli, 217
strudel, Fontina cheese and ham, 146
stuffed courgette flowers, 230
stuffed courgettes, 120, 122
stuffed green olives, 228–9
stuffed tomatoes, 154–5
sugo al pomodoro, 14
supplì, 232–3
Swiss chard, 67, 99, 191, 193, 267
swordfish
    carpaccio with capers, 274
    pizzaiola, 152

tablecloths, 4, 7–8
tagliata of beef with truffle, 244
tagliolini with truffle and anchovies, 242
tart
    ricotta and cherry, 258–9
    spinach, ricotta and pine nut, 66–7
tartine with truffle butter, 241
Teroldego wine, 41
timballo of pasta with tomato, speck and
    aubergine, 63–4
tiramisù with vin santo, 207
tomato
    heirloom, rocket and carpaccio of mushroom
        salad, 91
    over-ripe, 17
    stuffed with saffron rice, 154–5
    tomato and chilli penne, 50
    tomato paste, 16
    tomato peperonata, 221–2
    tomato sauce with hidden vegetables, 65
tonnarelli, 149, 279–80
torta rustica, 66–7
Trentino, 150
trofie with pesto and prawns, 185

Tropea red onion, pancetta and potato frittata, 169
truffle see october truffle celebrations
truffle butter, 241, 244
tuna
    rice salad with tuna and pickles, 167
    tuna tartare with citrus dressing, 275
Tuscan dessert wine, 28, 57, 207, 294

veal
    veal skewers with mortadella and sage, 316
    veal straccetti with sage and culatello di
        zibello, 90
    vitello tonnato, 297
vegetable soup with Altamura crostini, 53
vegetables, preserved, 198
vegetarian dishes, 18, 170
Venice, 60
Verona, 42
Vialone rice, 17, 117, 154–5
vin santo, 28, 57, 207, 294
vitello tonnato, 297
Vov, 275, 276

walnut, prune and pancetta caramels, 84
water, 14
white asparagus, 183
white pizza, 70
wild boar stracotto, 253
wild hare, 116
wines, 117
women's day mimosa dinner, 95–7
    aubergine parmigiana, 105
    crudités with pinzimonio and bagna cauda, 98
    kiwi, pistachio and feta salad, 106
    mimosa cake, 107–8
    orecchiette with broccoli rabe, Italian sausage
        and fennel fronds, 99–100
    risotto with smoked salmon, asparagus and
        lemon, 102–3

Zio Mario's eggs and peas, 54